THE WRITE BRIDGE

| MIND THE GAP |

A Biannual Literary Journal

Copyright © 2024 by Anamcara Press LLC
https://anamcara-press.com/the-write-bridge-zine/
Published biannually
Subscriptions: https://anamcara-press.com/subscribe-to-the-journal/
Cover Artword by Barbara Waterman Peters
Book design by Maureen Carroll
Editors Maureen Carroll, Amber Fraley
Arial, Tomarik, Lato, Professor Minty
Printed in the United States of America.

Book description: 2023 Journal anthology

This periodical is devoted to literature in a broad sense, publishing short stories, poetry, plays, and essays, along with book reviews, biographical profiles of authors, interviews and occasional letters. The essays in this journal are works of creative nonfiction. The fiction in this journal are products of the author's imaginations or are used fictitiously and are not to be construed as real. Any resemblance to actual events, locales, organizations or persons, living or dead, is entirely coincidental.

Published by
ANAMCARA PRESS LLC
P.O. Box 442072, Lawrence, KS 66044
https://anamcara-press.com

Ordering Information: Quantity sales. Special discounts are available on quantity purchases for libraries, bookstores, and others. For details, contact the publisher at the address above.

CATALOGING DATA:
THE WRITE BRIDGE JOURNAL / Perilous & Playful / Issue 5: Summer 2023
[edited by] Maureen Carroll [and] Amber Fraley [and] Ronda Miller

ISBN-13: The Write Bridge Journal WINTER 2023/2024, 978-1-960462-44-2
ISSN: Pending
LCO010000 LITERARY COLLECTIONS / Essays
LCO020000 LITERARY COLLECTIONS / Interviews
HUM003000 HUMOR / Form / Essays
BIO026000 BIOGRAPHY & AUTOBIOGRAPHY / Personal Memoirs

"Solitude is the soil in which genius is planted, creativity grows, and legends bloom; faith in oneself is the rain that cultivates a hero to endure the storm, and bare the genesis of a new world, a new forest."

— Mike Norton, White Mountain

Our mission is to spark wonder. *The Write Bridge* is published twice a year and features enthralling poetry, short fiction, and creative nonfiction.

THE WRITE BRIDGE

| *MIND THE GAP* |

A Biannual Literary Journal

SELECT WORKS OF NON-FICTION, POETRY, FICTION & ART

ISSUE #6; WINTER 2023/2024

SOLITUDE and SOLIDARITY

Anamcara Press LLC | Lawrence, Kansas

PREVIOUS ISSUES OF THE WRITE BRIDGE

THE WRITE BRIDGE | MIND THE GAP | SUMMER 2023
JOURNAL ISSUE #5
Theme: Perilous and Playful

THE WRITE BRIDGE | MIND THE GAP | FALL 2022
JOURNAL ISSUE #4
Theme: Fortitude and Pusillanimity

THE WRITE BRIDGE | MIND THE GAP | SPRING 2022
JOURNAL ISSUE #3
Theme: Heartbreak And Desire

THE WRITE BRIDGE | MIND THE GAP | FALL 2021
JOURNAL ISSUE #2
Theme: Isolation And Emergence

THE WRITE BRIDGE | MIND THE GAP | SPRING 2021
JOURNAL ISSUE #1
Authors explore the topic of inclusion, and offer up
some pandemic prose

WELCOME TO
THE WRITE BRIDGE JOURNAL

In each edition of *The Write Bridge,* readers are encouraged to "mind the gap" as writers and artists with powerful voices explore topics that broaden our thinking.

In a 1936 *Esquire* article entitled "The Crack Up," author F. Scott Fitzgerald wrote:

> *"Before I go on with this short history, let me make a general observation—the test of a first-rate intelligence is the ability to hold two opposed ideas in the mind at the same time, and still retain the ability to function. One should, for example, be able to see that things are hopeless and yet be determined to make them otherwise. This philosophy fitted on to my early adult life, when I saw the improbable, the implausible, often the 'impossible,' come true."*

The Write Bridge presents two opposing ideas for creators and readers to delve into—seriously or in fun—in order stretch our imaginations, to move beyond boundaries, to bridge the gap.

We hope the themes for *The Write Bridge* Journal Winter 2023/2024 edition, *Solitude* and *Solidarity,* will inspire, enlighten, and entertain you.

THE WRITE BRIDGE JOURNAL STAFF

Meet the team!

Anamcara Press LLC was founded by Maureen "Micki" Carroll in 2014 in celebration of art and community, and in support of authors and artists in their creative endeavors.

Carroll is a writer, educator, graphic designer, and all around cat herder. Her first book, *A Wyoming Cowboy in Hitler's Germany* combines war era correspondence and 70 year old photographs to depict an age of heroism and innocence. *The Tree Who Walked Through Time* was published in collaboration with 17 artists, including crop artist Stan Herd. She is also the author of the middle-grade series, Jo & the School's Out Squad. Carroll Chairs the Kansas Authors Club District #2 in Lawrence.

Assistant Editor and Publicist, Amber Fraley is your typical Gen Xer suburban Kansas wife and mom of one who grew up a book nerd in a dysfunctional family and now writes about those experiences as hilarious therapy. She's the author of the humorous essay collection *From Kansas, Not Dorothy*, and the viral essay "Gen X Will Not Go Quietly," as well as numerous human interest articles. Amber loves Kansas with all her heart, is frequently awkward in public, and desperately wishes to see a tornado and live to tell the tale.

Art/Design Editor, Kathleen (Kat) Williams is a multi-disciplinary artisan and scholar. Mythologist, metalsmith, seamstress, and songstress, Kat loves all things creative. With ample degrees in Arts and Culture she brings a diversified aesthetic to the publications of Anamcara Press. When she's not writing new myths or hand-crafting adornments, she's singing songs and helping other writers with their websites. You can find more about her and her work at www.tb3f.com

CONTRIBUTING VISUAL ARTISTS

Louis Copt has been painting professionally since 1976. He received a BA in art from Emporia State University in 1971, and also studied at the Art Students League of New York. He recently was the focus of a feature article in American Artist, which is based in New York and is one of the oldest art publications in the country. Collectors of Louis' work include the Kansas City Chiefs, H&R Block, Texas A&M, Federal Home Loan Bank, the University of Kansas, Kansas State University, the Overland Park Convention Center, CrossFirst Bank, and private collectors across the country. In 2011 he was named Governor's Artist by the Kansas Arts Commission.

Heather Duris is an artist living in Lawrence, Kansas. Heather makes jewelry, paints and has recently started making linocut prints. She is inspired by wild nature and the open landscapes of the prairie. Her style ranges from abstract landscapes to completely abstract expressions in color and shape. Her favorite artists include Henri Matisse, Helen Frankenthaler, Jean-Michel Basquiat and Raoul Dufy. heatherdurisart@gmail.com, facebook.com/HeatherDurisArt, Instagram.com/HeatherDurisArt, Heatherduris.substack.com

Cathy Martin is a mixed-media artist who lives and works on ten acres of woodland and meadow in the rolling hills of beautiful NE Kansas. Surrounded by the rich color and tapestry of the Colorado mountains and Iowa farmlands in her youth, landscapes are her specialty, and Cathy enjoys adding various wildlife into many of her paintings.

Ronda Miller is a Life Coach specializing in trauma. Miller teaches The Importance of Voice for Trauma Transformation in concert with The Johnson County Library, School of Trades and Department of Corrections. Her five books of poetry include: *Going Home: Poems from My Life*, *MoonStain*, *WaterSigns*, *Winds of Time* and *I Love the Child*.

Bobbie Powell attended KU and stayed in Lawrence, KS for 17 years creating, showing, and selling mixed media art, children book illustrations, drawings, and paintings. A member of art co-op groups Dot Dot Dot and Quintessential 5, Bobbie has had shows in Kansas City and Lawrence. She's done multiple commission projects including a solo show at the Great Plains Nature Center, painted two large outdoor murals and worked on children's book illustrations. Bobbie has painted murals in Ark City, KS, Lawrence, KS, Wichita, KS, Anthony, KS, and Kiowa KS. She is currently working on illustrating three books, one tattoo design, and one commission painting for a private residence.

Barbara Waterman-Peters, (BFA, Washburn University, MFA, Kansas State University, Honorary Doctor of Fine Arts, Washburn University) taught at Washburn and Kansas State Universities as well as for Lassen Community College in California. She has received a Certificate of Recognition for Outstanding Achievement from the State of Kansas and the Monroe Award from the Washburn University Alumni Association. In 2011 she was awarded the ARTY for Distinguished Visual Artist from ARTS Connect in Topeka. Her work has been included in more than 300 solo, group and juried exhibits. She is represented by several galleries, Jones in Kansas City, SNW in Manhattan, and Beauchamp in Topeka. She owns STUDIO 831 in the North Topeka Arts & Entertainment District (NOTO).

Garold Sneegas is a principal and cofounder of ColabDM Productions. Garold's primary role is the director of video and video production. Garold early photographic work was done with film. With the advent of digital photography his artistic Interests began exploring how far you can manipulate a digital image. This soon turned into how artistic can you get and can you turn it into another dimension. Garolds fascination with nature has been with him for as long as he can remember. His interest in nature led him to a Bachelor of Science Degree in Biology from Pittsburg State University in 1974. His interest in photography began in his high school and college years out of frustration of trying to express what he was seeing in nature verbally. This was especially true in regards to his greatest interest at that time freshwater aquatic flora and fauna.

CONTRIBUTING AUTHORS

Barry Barnes
Vern Barnet
Shelley Watts Barnhill
Stephanie A. Barrows
Lindsey Bartlett
Julie Ann Baker Brin
Patricia Cleveland
Ian Cook
Brian Daldorph
Anamarie Davis-Wilkins
Thaddeus Dugan
Heather Duris
Gretchen Cassel Eick
Andrew Evans
Robert Fraga
Amber Fraley
Beth Gulley
George Gurley

Duane L. Herrmann
D.A. Irsik
Kelly W. Johnston
Kathleen Kaska
Julia Mathias Manglitz
J.A. McGovern
Ronda Miller
Peg Nichols
Kevin Rabas
John Ritchie
Troy Robinson
Bruce Rolfe
Mark Scheel
Diane Silver
Lori Stratton
Connlyn Synclair
Chuck Warner
Barbara Waterman Peters
Brenda White

CONTENTS

PART III: TALL TALES, SHORT STORIES & ONE ACT PLAYS

INTRODUCTION:
THE SOLIDARITY WALL

Diary entry: I'm typing this from the Europa bar overlooking the street bustling with lines of stretch limos and throngs of tourists. The sirens have died away but a few police and fire trucks pull by once in a while. There is an air of excitement, probably generated by the tensions, or just Saturday night.

I flew to Belfast City last evening. Alone in a strange place, I was too tired to consider sightseeing. I did meet a nice fellow, Paul, at the airport and we shared a cab and had an interesting conversation. He gave me his card and I reciprocated. He believed he had some employees coming to my seminar. I asked about political correctness. He was very frank.

I later understood that he was open with me because of the taxi queue I'd elected to wait in. There were two lines—I picked one randomly, not knowing. People who DO know understand that one taxi is favored by Republicans (or Nationalists) and one taxi by Loyalists. It is just unspoken. Irish taxis are divided by color, corporation, and loyalty. Loyal to the Republic of Ireland versus loyal to Britain.

This is Northern Ireland (not England, not the Republic). Paul said there were still some problems, for example, a place where the Catholics abbreviate the name of the city, but the Protestants always use the name in full (Londonderry—Derry for the Republicans.) "You can't win. Whatever you say, you'll make someone angry," he said. (Although, later, the black-taxi tour driver said one could call it "the Maiden city" without causing themselves trouble with the troubles.)

I was getting an education in sectarianism. The *Oxford English Dictionary* defines "sectarianism" as, "a narrow-minded adherence to a particular sect (political, ethnic, or religious), often leading to conflict with those of different sects or possessing different beliefs." Sectarianism typically ends in serious ugliness ranging from prejudice and discrimination to violence and warfare.

Wikipedia lists several examples of sectarianism around the world. Conspicuously missing is the United States. Folks in the U.S. have believed themselves to be free of sectarianism due, in part, to our exceptional constitution. But sectarianism is undeniably creeping in as demonstrated by growing social and political polarization in the U.S. today.

Solidarity is something completely different from sectarianism. Solidarity is all about unity—inclusiveness, cooperation, and mutual support. Solidarity involves a sense of shared purpose and collective action in pursuit of common goals.

Germany tried to erase their hate-filled past unsuccessfully, but they did manage to get hate symbols out of the public

THE SOLIDARITY WALL AT THE FALLS ROAD

square through solidarity. It is illegal in Germany today to display Nazi symbols. But Germany's "enduring confrontation with the past" requires acknowledging their history openly and frequently in hopes of preventing its reoccurrence. (Yuliya Komska, *The Washington Post, https://www.washingtonpost. com/news/made-by-history/wp/2017/08/17/what-to-do-with-confederate-monuments-seven-lessons-from-germany/.)*

Through words and writing, through artwork and graffiti, sectarianism is communicated and spreads.

I'd selected from a handful of Belfast tourist brochures to take the Black Taxi tour—a 'political tour.' I'd heard about the murals at The Falls Road and wanted to go and see them in the afternoon, but when I called to make the arrangements, I was told, "The gates are closed this afternoon, so we'll have to go in the morning. There's a march."

The Protestant Orange were marching, still celebrating the victories of Cromwell (dead hundreds of years), and the Catholics were mourning their dead and reacting in their own ways to keep the hate alive. The "gates" (military barricades) were closed, literally dividing the city in an effort to reduce violence.

The tour consisted of myself and the tour guide—a taxi driver born and raised in the conflict. He had a great knowledge of "the Troubles" and did his best to remain politically correctly in the middle, however the murals speak for themselves.

The taxi driver insisted the current divisions in Northern Ireland are "mostly created by the working classes." Others have a vested interest in prosperity—meaning tourism and business travelers and investors who do not appreciate violence or extremism.

The Protestant Orange were marching, still celebrating the victories of Cromwell (dead hundreds of years)...

Paul's words came back to me and I repeated them to the cabbie, "Is it true there's been no conflict for over 10 years?"

The cabbie said there had been no "serious conflict" but two years ago, while business investors with deep pockets were in town, another Orange march had touched off hostilities and the investors had fled taking their money with them.

The town looked battered with graffiti, and the murals tell a troubled tale. The term "Troubles" refers to the period of time in Belfast between the early 1960s and the 1998 Good Friday Accord negotiated by U.S. President Bill Clinton. The violence of the "Troubles" was worsened because the British government and military colluded with the Loyalists against the Republicans. Violence between the mostly Protestant "Loyalists," who wish to remain united with Great Britain, and the mostly Catholic "Republicans," who wish to be part of the Republic of Ireland, continues to this day. In spite of the religious divisions, Northern Ireland's sectarianism is seen as political rather than religious.

The loyalist murals are very brutal and depict scenes of violent overthrow—William of Orange in 1690, hooded men with AK 47 rifles, depictions that look like something from a war zone. The Republican murals, instead, are mostly memorials to the dead—little gardens with names displayed and fresh flowers. I saw only one violent mural on the Republican side, an historical mural memorializing the burning of Catholic Belfast in 1969. The contrast was striking.

The cabbie said "dogs on the street" were talking and violent reactions were likely in response to the Orange march set to happen that afternoon. The Twelfth, or Orangeman's Day, celebrates the victory of Protestant King William of Orange over Catholic King James II at the Battle of the Boyne in 1690.

If you're thinking that is a long time to celebrate something, you're right. The march and the murals keep alive old wounds under the auspices of celebrating history, like statues of Confederate heros standing in American town squares.

> Sectarianism doesn't grow like a wild flower in a field. It's in a window box, it's in a potting shed, it's nurtured, it's fed, and it's passed on generation to generation.
> —David Erving

"The majority of us," the cabbie said, "could care less about the extremists on either side and just want to get on with our life."

And so it is for the majority of us elsewhere in the world. Most people are not extremists. Most of us just want to get on with our life free from hatred and violence.

In Northern Ireland today people are working together to repaint the murals. This is not an effort to white-wash their history, but rather a way to avoid provoking future hatred. They are coming together in solidarity to paint pictures of sports victories rather than violence.

Instead of sectarianism, when I looked at the murals at The Falls Road, Belfast, also known as "The Solidarity Wall,"

I saw a creative act of cooperation in boldly colored paint—a collection of artwork expressing support for global causes. Art as an act of unity.

Solidarity is inclusive, cooperative, and unifying. Through words and writing, through artwork and music, solidarity is communicated and spreads. Writers and artists mirror society—they illustrate our short-comings, and also lead the way in defining where we are going and give us a vision of a brighter future.

Solitude is the soil—the medium of artistic creation. An author or artist creates in solitude. In solitude the seed germinates. Just as the sun pulls the sprout to the surface, the author or artist—through their creation—pulls us toward each other and our common values. In solitude the musician finds the common chord, then sings our solidarity into being.

The lyrics we harmonize along with, the films that awe us, the authors whose words reverberate long after we've read them—these creative acts unify us. We owe a debt of gratitude to those whose voices and visions, cultivated in solitude, bring us together in solidarity.

Barry "Washboard" Barnes is one such voice. A poet and musician, Barry finds the common chord. Featured in "Interview With An Author," Barry recommends we, "Make the most of every moment" in his poem, "Use It Or Lose It." He says, "For me, everything is poetry. It's all poetry."

Barbara Waterman Peters is an artist and writer with a skill of bringing opposites together. "The act of creating allows a portal into another realm, another dimension which is often called 'the zone,'" Barbara reminds us in, "Interview With An Artist." When you're in the zone, "There is no time, no pain, no awareness of the physical world. What is there is the freedom to explore all sorts of possibilities and even some impossibilities."

Contributors to this edition of *The Write Bridge* explore and bring together the opposing topics SOLITUDE and SOLIDARITY in poetry and prose, offering the reader opportunity for reflection and perhaps an ah ha moment.

The following articles, poems, stories, and plays demonstrate the power of words to lift us above differences, to find a common chord, and to soothe our collective spirit. They show how writers and artists can expose wounds and also provide a salve to comfort.

The desire to let go of someone or something and the desire to hold on are both explored within these pages. If you strive to hold on, consider Lindsey Bartlett's, "Someone Lived There" or D.A. Irsik's, "Unbreakable Bond."

If you prefer release, check out, "A Murder At Radius," by Brenda White, or "Garden of Eden/Eatin," by Kevin Rabas.

Both solitude and solidarity are explored in "Friendship Fountain," by Peg Nichols and "Noticing Solitude and Sanctuary," by Gretchen Cassel Eick.

Peruse the works within, and you may forge bonds of solidarity with the contributing authors and artists—even as we read and write alone, together, in solitude.

—*Maureen (Micki) Carroll, Editor-in-chief*

In solitude the musician finds the common chord,
then sings our solidarity into being.

Etymology

The featured word for this issue's
etymology review is:

SOLIDARITY

from Latin: *solidus* "firm, whole, undivided, entire,"
"ON BEHALF OF THE WHOLE"

From the French: *solide* "solid"
solidaire "interdependent, complete, entire,"
solidarité "mutual good understanding"

"The fact or quality on the part of communities,
etc., of being perfectly united
or at one in some respect"

"Perfect coincidence of (or between) interests." 1890

"TRUST IN EACH OTHER"

*"communion of interests and responsibilities, mutual
responsibility,"—the "Encyclopédie" (1765).*

Definitions from the *Compact Edition of the Oxford English Dictionary,* **Oxford University Press 1971, and** *Dictionary of Word Origins,* **John Ayto, Arcade Publishing 1990.**

MAUREEN CARROLL, PHOTO

PART I:
ARTICLES & ESSAYS

WEAVING IT ALL TOGETHER

Featured articles submitted for the Winter 2023/2024 edition of *The Write Bridge* range from the nostalgic to the satirical. Have you left something behind? Bartlett explores the haunting solitude of abandoned structures in, "Somebody Lived There." Have you found yourself unexpectedly alone? Irsik delves into the bonds created in good and bad times in, "Unbreakable Bond." Have you risked putting your views on the line? Andrew Evans explores the ramifications of asking the boss to proof-read a leaflet exposing his own shenanigans in, "No Respect For the Union Professionals," and more. Enjoy!

BARRY "WASHBOARD" BARNES

Interview With An Author:
Barry "Washboard" Barnes

— *by Amber Fraley*

AF: Of all the vehicles available for expression, why do you choose poetry?

BWB: I think in my late teens and early twenties, I thought I would write songs, but I wasn't a skilled musician—I didn't play guitar or anything, so I couldn't play my own songs—and I really wasn't good enough to sing a cappella, so I started taking the words to poetry readings and reading them. So, then I thought— maybe I'm a poet.

AF: When did you learn that words have power?

BWB: The first thing I learned was how I can use my voice in certain tones to like, get my dog to behave—just the power of my voice.

My first-grade teacher, Miss Daphne Harris—I had trouble reading, and she was friends with my mom, so sometimes I'd go to her house and she'd work with me. She had a Dr. Seuss book—something about a poodle in a bottle eating noodles—it always stuck with me.

AF: (I looked up the book Barry referenced, and following is the passage he remembers.)

"When beetles fight these battles in a bottle with their paddles and the bottle's on a poodle and the poodle's eating noodles... they call this a muddle puddle tweetle poodle beetle noodle bottle paddle battle."
— Dr. Seuss, Fox in Socks

AF: Who are your influences?

BWB: My big influence early on was probably Frank Zappa.

When I heard the *Apostrophe* album, that taught me it's okay to draw outside the lines. Right now, I'm really into Joanna Newsome. Most of her songs are memorized poems—and they're really long—she got into it because she took a college class about book-long poems and she'd memorize them. If you listen to her songs, she'll be reciting a poem in the song for like five or ten minutes.

AF: It seems as though there's more emphasis on spoken word for you than just the written word.

BWB: Yeah. Because I don't know how well my written word translates without the intonations. I'm not a very good reader. That's really why I started committing my stuff to memory. So I could do my poems without stumbling over the words and things like that. Then I realized that once they were in my head, I could play with them.

AF: Oh, do you change the way you perform them?

BWB: Yeah, I will. I will change a poem if something pops in my head. I'll throw an extra word in, or cater to the audience or say something different if there are children in the room, and things like that. Words are malleable.

AF: I think every time I've ever seen you perform your poetry you've used a drum. Do you always perform poetry with a drum?

BWB: Um, no. I actually do a lot of poetry without anything... and I've been using this a lot, now. (Barry gestures to his electronic keyboard and looping rig.) For MLK day I took it down to the library and did some poetry with it.

AF: Is there anything special about your writing process?

BWB: Sometimes things just come to me, and I'll write them down. But if I want to write and nothing's happening, I can make that happen by reading other people's poetry, or reading a book, watching a movie... Or music. If I hear a song, during the guitar solo I'll hear words instead of each individual string. It'll be talking to me.

AF: What would you say is the most difficult part of writing?

BWB: If I want to write something and nothing's coming, that can be difficult. Or sometimes I'll share something and think later that maybe I shouldn't have shared it.

AF: How many poems do you have memorized? Do you have any idea?

BWB: At one point, including other people's poetry, I probably had 300 poems that I could recite off the top of my head. Now that's probably down to 99, and that's just my poetry—and some Langston Hughes stuff.

AF: Who are some of your favorite poets?

BWB: Definitely Langston Hughes. Maya Angelou. Walt Whitmann. Who's the old Scottish guy? He wrote Auld Lang Syne... Robert Burns. Gail Scott Harris.

AF: What's something surprising you've learned about yourself through the writing process?

BWB: I'm generally writing about the person I want to be. I use it for direction.

For me, everything is poetry. It's all poetry. Like wordplay. Wordsmithing. I have to do that. It's the reason for all the puns I post (on social media) and the jokes I come up with. My brain is just constantly doing that. If someone says something my brain will take it and reprocess it into something else—you can do this with it, you can do that with it.

AF: Did it surprise you to find out that people wanted to listen to your poetry?

BWB: Yeah. It was surprising. So many people do it—are out there writing. I know when I do it live, people tend to like it. I'm not so sure about when they read my writing—because it's open to interpretation, I guess. People will come to me and say, 'You meant this,' and I'll be like, okay. If that's what you heard and saw, I guess that's what it means, then. But it does depend on the poem. I might turn around and say 'No, actually, this is exactly what this means.'

AF: Do you hide any secrets in your poems that only a few people will find?

BWB: I know that if I make a Frank Zappa reference, or a Jimi Hendrix reference, or a reference from a cartoon, certain people will pick up on that. Cartoons have had a big impact on me.

AF: Do you view writing as a kind of spiritual practice?

BWB: Yes. It's cathartic. Spiritual. I wouldn't say I'm a religious person, but spiritual, yeah.

AF: Is it something you do every day?

BWB: I was in the 365 group. I did it for two years. What I'm doing now, with music and stuff, drives that. I'll make a loop and I'll find words that go to it. I'll go through my archives and try to find something or I'll write something new. I've been looping for about 20 years now, but I just recently started sharing them.

AF: How did the looping add to your poetry or change it?

BWB: For a while, I would find some cool instrumentals—hip hop or dance music or rock or whatever—and I would use those as backing tracks at poetry readings sometimes. What this did (gesturing to the keyboard) was make it so I could make my own backing tracks.

AF: Do you try to be more original, or traditional with your poetry?

BWB: I try to mix them. But there's too many rules with tradition. I like drawing outside the lines. There was a poet who came to my church when I was a kid and her book was called "I Don't Punctuate." I liked that. I'll do stuff like write a poem, and I'll like the way the words look on the paper, so I'll keep it.

AF: Do you have relationships with other authors? How do you support each other?

BWB: I work with BLACK Lawrence, and we're all poets and authors. We support each other by showing up to the performances so there's someone in the audience if no one shows up. And we encourage each other, patting each other on the back and pushing forward... finding gigs for each other. Things like that. Alex (Kimball Williams) is really good at finding us places to perform.

AF: What does writing success look like to you?

BWB: You know, if I do a poetry reading and one person from the audience comes up and says "I liked this because of that," I've done my job.

So So Small:
Barry "Washboard" Barnes

Here we aren't
In a universe so vast
We have already
Come and gone
Our precious lives
Some hold so dear
Most take for granted
Are but silent echoes
So enjoy the ride
Take it all in
For it is
Incomprehensibly brief

Barry R. Barnes Peace
7/14/2022 12:02pm.

(Use It Or Lose It):
Barry "Washboard" Barnes

Take some time to enjoy the day
Never know what's coming your way
Open your eyes look around
Open your ears take in the sound
Share some hugs hold some hands
If you don't like something take a stand
Do not be afraid to love
Try not to waste any time on hate
Because the time you have is all the time you've got
What I'm trying to say is there's not a lot
Try to make the most of every moment
Some times Happiness is a choice
Use it or lose it

Barry R. Barnes Peace
4/28/2011 5:12pm

BARRY WASHBOARD BARNES is a published poet, professional washboard and rubboard player, loop artist, performance artist, and percussionist. Born in Lawrence, Kansas, Barry has been living and performing in and around the Lawrence area for more than 40 years. Barry has one book of poetry published, *We Sleep in a Burning House,* and is currently working on second book of poetry. Barry also performs solo and with the Zydeco Tougeau Duo out of Lawrence, and the Ernest James Zydeco Band out of Kansas city.

GAROLD SNEEGAS, PHOTO

Funerals Could Be Better:
Amber Fraley

Recently, I attended a funeral for a friend. His death was sudden, and a shock to all of us. I spent the week after the announcement of his death mourning my friend and dreading the funeral.

I hate funerals. It's a human ritual I'd rather avoid, but of course must occasionally participate in, not for me, but for other people — to show my respect and love not just for the person who has died, but for the friends and family left behind who also loved them.

What I don't like about funerals — in America, anyway — is the impersonality and unnecessarily morbid tone of so many traditional ceremonies. How often have we all sat through funerals where a pastor who clearly never met the deceased person orates a eulogy that doesn't even begin to do the person justice? I understand it's a difficult time for family or friends to speak about the deceased, especially when the death is sudden, but there's usually someone who's up to the task.

A few years ago when a friend of mine lost her dad, her husband gave a beautiful tribute himself, but he also read a letter their youngest daughter wrote about her Grandpa. It was the most touching part of the service, and everyone chuckled at the granddaughter's declaration that one thing she'd remember about her Grandpa was how he "put gravy on everything."

Those are the human moments we treasure and want to remember.

As an atheist, it drives me crazy when a fellow atheist dies, but the family insists on a religious funeral, which of course, is for the benefit of the family, not the deceased. Religious people always assume this is okay and not hurting anyone, but I find it incredibly disrespectful, and honestly, it ends up making me angry in addition to being sad. It's as if everything my friend or loved one stood for didn't mean anything and can be completely dismissed. I understand religious people may be dismayed if God is left out of the funeral ceremony completely, but it seems to me that including a religious element could be handled in a less insulting manner to others' beliefs.

And when I say funerals tend to be morbid, I'm not saying funerals shouldn't have room for sadness. Of course, they should. Anyone should feel free to bawl their eyes out at a funeral and that's a perfectly appropriate response.

But laughter is also okay at a funeral. Good thoughts and remembrances are more than okay. Funerals should have room for celebration as well as sorrow. Funerals should be a time to come together and give tribute to the individual we've lost, and all the wonderful qualities we'll miss about them.

On an even more personal note, I don't think the body or the urn must be displayed at every funeral. I have heard people say they need to see a body or urn for closure. I prefer to remember the person as they were in life, as opposed to my last memory being of their lifeless body or a faceless container. That's not to say I'm offended by bodies at funerals—I'm not, and I'm sympathetic to other people's need to include them as part of the ceremony.

My friend's funeral was okay. No one spoke at all—which was disappointing—but there were photos of him playing on a loop and it was like a wake, with everyone chatting, making new acquaintances, and telling stories about our recently departed friend and loved one. That part was lovely.

But honestly, none of it needed to even be at a funeral home. It would've been fabulous if they'd reserved a private room at one of my friend's favorite local restaurants where we could snack, drink, and reminisce while some of his favorite '80s tunes had been playing along with his photos, no urn required, because in some way, it might've felt as if he were there with us.

I miss you, friend.

AMBER FRALEY, author of *Kansas GenExistential* and *The Bug Diary,* is your typical Gen Xer Kansas wife and mom of one who grew up a book nerd in a dysfunctional family and now writes about those experiences as hilarious therapy. She's the author of *From Kansas, Not Dorothy*, and the viral essay **"Gen X Will Not Go Quietly,"** as well as numerous human interest articles. Amber loves Kansas, is frequently awkward in public, and desperately wishes to see a tornado and live to tell the tale.

"If your body and soul instinctively know exactly when the drum solo kicks in for Jack and Diane, then you will want to read this book. Amber Fraley's *Kansas Genexistential* is an homage to a broad-minded, affirming Midwest culture where bigotry and patriarchy can go suck on a chili dog."

-Nathan Pettengill
editor, Sunflower Publishing

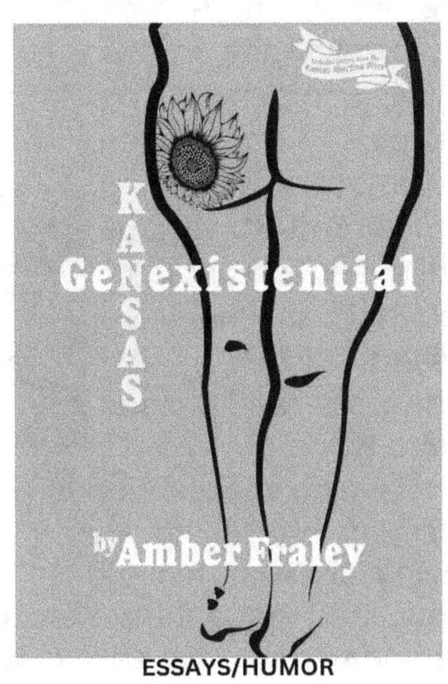

Someone Lived There:
Lindsey Bartlett

"She loves old things; the history attached with dilapidated structures. The strugglers of life have a soul she says."

-Avijeet Das

The house is weathered, stripped of paint. Broken or missing windows have let in wildlife, dirt, and debris. The Kansas wind has torn shingles from the roof, allowing for holes. A chimney is missing bricks. Inside is stained carpet, peeling and faded wallpaper, things left behind. A rodent-eaten chair or mattress. An old stove or washtub. The barn and other outbuildings tell of a similar fate. Of a time when there was once fresh hay in the hayloft, horses in the stables, and the equipment of a working farm stored in various nooks and crannies. A time that has long since passed this old farmstead and many others by.

LINDSEY BARTLETT, PHOTO

I have no specific time or event that led to my fascination with the old farmsteads that dot the Kansas prairie; it is an interest I feel in some ways I have always had. I think anyone who lives in rural areas of Kansas are familiar with the many abandoned homes and farmsteads that dot the countryside. Many folks probably pass by these places paying little attention to a property in a continuous state of decay. These properties are just another part of the landscape, of little interest for those on their way to somewhere else.

These abandoned homesteads that dot our prairie landscape show the decline in rural America. In a way of life that is no longer seen as sustainable as it once was. They are symbols of a time gone by. A time when small family farms played a much bigger role in agriculture before "go big or get out" became the mantra surrounding agriculture in the 1960s. A time when farming was a primary method of income and survival for families and rural communities.

However, these abandoned homesteads are more than just symbols for rural decline and a bygone lifestyle. At one time these homes housed families. Folks not all that different from you and me, who went through many of the same things we do today, from births to marriage, holiday gatherings, and the death of loved ones.

A teacher by trade, one of my hobbies is photography, and among my favorite things to photograph are abandoned homesteads. As I explore and photograph these old places, I can't help but imagine what they might have looked like when some unknown individuals called them home. What did the house look like with a brand-new coat of paint and curtains fluttering in the window? Did the family sit outside on nice evenings and watch the sun make its slow decline behind the horizon? Maybe they watched lightning bugs at dusk and prayed for rain for the crops.

Sometimes these old farmsteads are hard to see from the roadside. The trees and brush have grown up around them, nature taking back what is rightfully its own. The only signs that someone once lived there may be a rusted mailbox sitting crooked on wooden pole, its lid hanging open, having not seen a letter or a bill in years maybe even decades. Maybe there is a no trespassing sign hanging on a fence, spray painted on an old tire. Warning those who come to vandalize or steal that this is not their property, keep out! Keeping out those like me who would do no harm, but rather want to document what is left of another's past life. As the Miranda Lambert song, "The House that Built Me" says, "If I could come in, I swear I'll leave/won't take nothin' but a memory." The places that are fenced off and overgrown hold the most mystery to me, and also the most sadness. Someone cares enough to fence it off, lock the gate, put up a sign, but not enough to keep the buildings from decay.

As a kid, I had an hour-long bus ride to school every day, and in those early mornings not yet awake enough to do much else, I would stare out the window. I have always had an overactive imagination (probably why I am a writer now), and so as I stared out the window of the big yellow school bus, I would often imagine various things. Part of my imaginings included an abandoned homestead along the highway. It was up on a steep incline (not really a hill), and the trees were starting to overtake it. However, you could still see parts of a house standing, a windmill, and an outbuilding. In all honesty, as a kid, with the early morning sunlight just starting to shine through the trees casting eerie shadows, it was kind of creepy looking. At some point the house caught on fire, leaving behind nothing but stone ruins, and the old creaking windmill.

Years after the fire, my dad and I decided to go exploring while out taking photos. There isn't much left except for a stone wall that at one time must have been part of a gorgeous old house. Part of the wall still standing contains a hole where a stove pipe might once have gone, providing heat to the family who lived there during a cold Kansas winter. Maybe they huddled around this stove on a cold Christmas morning, while the children opened gifts. If each of those stones could talk, each one would have plenty of stories to tell about the people who called the place home over the decades.

In photographing these old homes, I have often noticed the juxtaposition of old and new. At one particular farmstead my dad and I visited, the outbuildings and the house were in a pretty serious state of decay stripped of paint, missing windowpanes, etc., however, on a couple sides the house was sporting what appeared to be almost brand-new storm windows. As if someone had thought about fixing the place up, but something, maybe time or money or even death had intervened.

Like all of us with our many scars and flaws, these homesteads are more than just rotted wood and broken glass, the long-forgotten stories of the individuals that lived there are etched into the remaining walls. Growing up, one of the upstairs rooms in our old farmhouse was covered in various writing, artwork, and even a few brittle posters of puppies and kittens from the family who had lived there several decades before. We used this room for storage, and I would often find myself peering around the boxes of Christmas décor or the leftover items from the pet and craft store my parents had once owned, to try to see more of what had been written on the wall. The word smile always stood out in brightly colored bubble letters. Before my parents and I moved in 2000, I took a pink pen to those walls and etched my own name. Something to say I was there.

LINDSEY BARTLETT teaches composition and literature at Emporia State University. Bartlett's poetry can be found in her book, *Vacant Childhood.* Additional writings and photography have appeared in The Milk House: A Rural Writing Collective, The Write Bridge, Flint Hills Review, and 105 Meadowlark Reader.

Subscribe to *The Write Bridge* Biannual Literary Journal

https://anamcara-press.com/
subscribe-to-the-journal/

CATHY MARTIN, OIL ON CANVAS

Unbreakable Bond:
D.A. Irsik

Sometimes solidarity is born of necessity, and my dependence on my siblings was that kind of bond. Our parents divorced when we were small, and my mother took us to my Grandma and Grandpa Fosdick's house while my mother was finding herself. My mother was only about twenty-five and had four young kids, so this entailed several men drifting in and out of our lives.

Bud owned a motel. Often mom would take us to the motel where, I think she might have been working, and she would leave us in one of Bud's rooms. It had a small kitchen, and we experimented with cooking, mostly dusting it with flour and various other explorations. Bud was not fond of us. We were generally left to our own devises, and we took care of each other.

My little sister was a climber, and we tried to keep her on our radar but sometimes we would find her on a counter. One such time, she ingested an entire bottle of baby aspirin and had to get her stomach pumped. My oldest sister, Linda, was probably about seven and a half, so not an age for the kind of responsibility that went with taking care of a six-year-old brother, five-year-old sister and two-and-a-half-year-old toddler. We did not see Bud again after the incident.

Mom disappeared for a while and came back married to a man named Gib. He had slicked-back hair and scars on his face that he told us he got from being in a plane crash in the war. I think they were actually acne scars.

Gib could be fun, but more often than not, he and my mother had very physical arguments. Gib had a drinking problem and would get mean. We were living in a little house about two streets up from Grandma and Gramps. Gib was a horse trainer by trade and he was working for Sunnyslope farm. We would get to go out and watch him and the other trainers work with the high trotting harness horses. We even got to meet The Lemon Drop Kid. Lemon Drop had been on the cover of Sports Illustrated in November 1957 and we got to see him in his stall and even pet him on a good day.

Those were the good times. They were rare. Gib lost his job at Sunnyslope and my grandmother got the school to give him a chance as a custodian. This was good and bad because he seemed to resent my mom for it. One night, they got into such a horrific fight that we snuck out and walked to Grandma and Grandpa's house. Not such a big deal, except Gib told us he would beat us, and he broke the window out of the front door by slamming it hard when he was yelling at us. We waited until he and my mother had quit screaming, and it got quiet, and then we snuck out in the snow and walked in our PJs to Grandma and Grandpa's house. Glenny was crying because she was barefoot, so Rick carried her on his back.

When I was in second grade, Mom and Gib woke us in the middle of the night and loaded us up and took us to Wichita.

Our experiences there included being left alone for two to three days while Mom and Gib went to horse shows in Kansas City. The motel we lived in was on the river and we would go down and collect mussels and put them in our bathroom sink. We thought they were oysters, and we hoped to discover a pearl. We found an old tire tube and floated around on the river, never realizing the danger. I don't know why the owner of the place didn't call social services, but she would ask us where our parents were and give us Cokes. I think mom probably left us with bread and bologna. We depended on each other more than we ever depended on adults to take care of us. We lived in a house in Wichita for a short time, and then Gib took us to St. Charles, Missouri.

I was in the third grade, and we were on our own from the time we got off the bus until Mom came home from her job at the nursing home. I had not finished the end of my second-grade year, but somehow, I was in third grade. My brother and sisters and I were very close because we were all we had. We were a team. Oh, we fought like siblings do, but we took care of each another. There were so many times when I look back that I know I would not have survived if not for my siblings and our unbreakable bond.

DEBRA IRSIK retired from the beauty industry after over twenty-five years. She is a Kansas girl and shares her life with her husband Mike, and children John and Emily. Deb is a member of The Kansas Authors Club, and Emporia Writing Group. Her *Heroes by Design* Y.A. fiction series was completed in 2020 and she is dedicating her time to creating a book of poetry and writing essays, prose and fiction. Deb also has published works in 105 Meadowlark Reader and The Write Bridge. She was an Amity literary prize finalist in 2023. The contest is sponsored by Anamcara Press.

SUNSHINE IN THE WEEDS

Poetry that warms the heart in places where the sun forgot to shine.

With eloquent finesse, Irsik explores the bonds between mothers, friends, and nature. Inviting readers to discover the divine in life's smallest moments, Irsik provides a heartfelt connection to the human spirit to brighten the hidden corners.

In a collection dedicated to her younger self, D.A. Irsik shares words that evoke images of life, love, and belonging. ... a nostalgic look at how the simple parts of life are, in the end, most important. —*Curtis Becker, author of My Second Act and Greetings from Topeka.*

D. A. Irsik
https://dairsik.com,
https://facebook.com/
D.A.IrsikAuthor https://instagram.com/dairsik

HEATHER DURIS, BURNED FIELDS,
ACRYLIC 16X20X2, 2023

Connections:
Troy Robinson

Along a stretch of Kansas highway, slightly northwest of Maize and Wichita, sits in solitude a lone cottonwood tree. Its majestic silhouette, a landmark, towering against the limitless sky. It is widely known this tree is not just any tree, and while it stands alone, it is never lonely. Those who live in the area, or cross its path regularly, understand this is a very special tree. For any who will listen, we who recognize and understand, excitedly enlighten all whenever an opportunity arises.

Arborists believe this single cottonwood boasts an age exceedingly more than one hundred years. Standing silent witness, the tree has presided over life upon the south-central Great Plains of Kansas for more than a century. Labeled *Populus deltoides* by scientists, the locals and others "in the know," affectionately call the tree "Lucky" or "Honking." These affectionate endearments arose because this particular tree is imbued with a magick interwoven by thousands of hopeful travelers, who, in solidarity, honk their horns driving by. This display of respect is often borne from a desire for reciprocation, in the form of luck the tree may bestow upon them.

Early within its history, Kansas did not have many trees and a great number of spaces were completely devoid of such foliage. The very first trees were imported by settlers and farmers, with the cottonwood identified as the "pioneer tree of Kansas." As these grew, indigenous birds and animals began to spread the seeds, sowing additional trees. Soon towns, developers, and residents planted trees more freely. As the trees themselves became established, they stretched out their roots to propagate further, steadily emerging across the land. For the cottonwood specifically, the annual release of cotton tufts bearing small seeds to drift upon the winds enables the tree to colonize other areas. One can only wonder upon the series of entangled behaviors enabling Lucky to first sprout within the soil all those many years ago.

Without protection upon the plains, few solitary trees survive the high winds, blustering heat, heavy snow, or occasional tornadoes. Without the support and shelter of other trees or adjacent buildings, Lucky stands proudly, defying the harsh and unforgiving weather frequently ravaging our state. Fire and ice, lightning and floods, even malicious vandalism and highway construction – Lucky survives the dangers wrought by nature and the callousness of man – resolute and uncompromising, a witness to all. The energy surrounding this cottonwood is so inspiring, it has catapulted Lucky to fame and a social media following. A fitting example of a species named as the official state tree.

It is possible those passing by are just in need of every bit of luck they can muster, or, simply honking at a tree is a fun activity to do with your kids on the drive into town. For each their own, but I believe there is more to this relationship between an aged cottonwood and the numerous individuals and families who frequently pay it homage. That a solitary tree has united so many in solidarity is a testament to the importance of Nature interwoven throughout each of us. While undoubtedly Lucky represents different things to different people, each unique influence cannot be viewed in isolation, nor discounted as an important component of a greater whole. Imagining what Lucky has observed prompts us to contemplate the lives overseen and the struggles endured throughout the past century, further encouraging a deeper examination into our relationships and connection to one another. Perhaps then, Lucky motivates us to reflect upon our progress as a species, our accomplishments and failures, to identify what works and what no longer serves a purpose. Could this be the message Lucky communicates – to strive and survive as a community in spite of overwhelming adversity?

Passing by Lucky, our thoughts wander to colorful and adventurous stories to be shared – and more importantly –

lessons to be learned. We acknowledge Lucky's sovereignty and wisdom by honoring this beacon of resilience through the honk of a horn, and in doing so, we connect our commonality within a sea of diversity.

A Kansas native, TROY ROBINSON recently retired from State service. After nearly 40 years of technical instruction and writing involving lesson plans, training manuals, policies, and investigative reports, he is now exploring the world of creative writing. His poems "Legacy Lost" and "Glory" were published in *The Tulgey Wood*, Vol. 52, 2023. He is a member of the Kansas Author's Club, District 6. This is Troy's first published short-story.

Glendyn Buckley, Author, and Barbara Waterman-Peters, Author, Illustrator

BARBARA WATERMAN PETERS, "MWS: CAROUSEL"
OIL ON CANVAS

No Respect for Union Professionals:

Andrew Evans

I was working in Washington D.C. in the communications department of the AFL-CIO in the early 2000s when I met Rick, a person who used his law degree in a nontraditional way to help workers. He was disenchanted with what he saw, not only in corporate America but at his international union headquarters. Rick hated bureaucracy and wanted change. He left his high-paying and prestigious director of research job with the international union.

After wishing him safe travels, Rick replied, "Solidarity!" His new job was the one-person research director for a small union local in Colorado. Although he gets to make strategic decisions, not everybody realizes the impact that he has. Rick does not mind because he feels he is making a difference and seems very excited about what he calls his vocation.

A few months later, I was visiting family in Colorado and decided to spend the day with Rick at his new job. He had put together a collection of books to create his union local's law library. It was similar to what one would have for a sole law practitioner. They were stored in bookcases in a small office room. However, in place of traditional law treatises a lot of the books were NOLO (no contest) publications, which are designed for the layperson. Rick explained how NOLO publications were practical enough for his needs, and how he did not need a lot of legal theory.

The employees and members of his local were allowed to check out books by simply writing down their names and contact information on a note pad hanging on the wall. Rick did not have any cataloging training, but the books were organized by subject. Rick also had copies of a few books in his office that nobody could check out. These included the Colorado Revised Statutes and various labor law publications.

Rick said the electronic databases he subscribed to was where his "real work took place." His biggest focus is on investigating individuals. "Sometimes it's a simple matter of locating a worker. Companies don't have a legal obligation to share where their workers live. Thus I use the professional version of KnowX.com."

Rick went on to explain how important it is to locate a worker's home. This allows union organizers to make a home visit and discuss the benefits of a union. "Employers do not allow an open discussion about unionization at the workplace and bombard workers with anti-union messages throughout an organizing drive," Rick said.

Rick showed me an example of how KnowX.com works. He handed me a list of workers' names a union organizer handed him. He then showed me a list he compiled with lots of personal information added including the social security numbers of those workers. Rick even listed the names of spouses and neighbors. It was very intrusive!

I asked Rick if the company provided the workers' names and Rick just laughed. Rick said, "Companies don't give us anything, not even names! What often happens is a union organizer acts as a customer and uses the rest room. Then he pokes around until he finds the time clock. That's when he pulls out a piece of paper and starts writing down all the listed names."

I asked Rick if he handled the legal work for the local. "No, I'm not licensed to practice law," Rick said. I asked why not, and Rick explained how a law license would not allow him to do his job effectively because some of his work might result in sanctions.

Rick continued, "As a research director for a progressive union local, I have to use information in unique ways. I do not break the law, but much of what I do seems unethical. Licensed attorneys are and should be ethical. My main goal is to get people and organizations to change their behavior. I just do what works without breaking the law." He then put in a CD of Judas Priest playing "Breaking The Law."

Rick proceeded to bring me up to date about the current labor strike at the Cheapskate Factory in Infinity, a small mountain town in Colorado.

"Sometimes when the company refuses to provide decent compensation, the workers have to go on strike. During this process, the company loses revenues while workers don't receive paychecks. It's often a matter of seeing who caves in first. Paradise bank was the only bank in town. After the first month of the strike, workers only had the strike fund to depend on for support. When car and house payments of striking workers were late or did not contain the full amount, Paradise Bank was quick to undergo repossession proceedings."

I asked Rick if this was normal and he responded, "Banks can provide a lot of leeway and don't mind sucking in the extra interest and fees from late payments resulting from labor disputes but Paradise Bank was not cutting any slack. I did a lot of research and made some Freedom of Information Act requests with the Federal Reserve."

Rick discovered how an executive of Cheapskate sat on Paradise Bank's board of directors. Even though it was interesting, Rick said this was not enough to use in changing the bank's behavior. So he did some more digging.

Rick said, "The Federal Reserve requires banks insured by it to disclose information about insider loans. These are loans provided to bank employees and board of directors. I did not find any dirt about the Cheapskate's executive, but I found lots of good information about other insiders through the state government's office of liens."

Rick asked me to design a leaflet directing bank customers to ask the bank president how they could obtain a two percent loan to buy a car just like bank director and Cheapskate Chief Operations Officer John Doe or how they can be excused from paying their mortgage for almost a year like director and Vice President of Finance Jane Doe.

Rick explained, "Imagine what little faith townsfolk would have in the bank's fairness if they knew about these sweetheart deals. They would probably drive thirty miles and bank elsewhere."

I told Rick that was an interesting way to use information. The leaflet I designed looked great! It was professional looking, direct, and to the point. Customers were asked to inquire about the preferred bank director status. Hopefully, the local media would share the leaflet and my skills would be noticed! Rick never needed to distribute the leaflet.

He took it to the bank president, told him he was an employee of the union, and asked him to proofread it for mistakes. The bank president said, "You can't pass this out."

"Why not? All the information is true." Rick replied.

"This is illegal. You are trying to blackmail me," countered the bank president. However, it wasn't blackmail because Rick claims it was not a threat. He merely asked the bank president to proofread the leaflet. The bank president asked Rick to wait in the lobby for a few minutes.

Rick said, "As I was leaving his office, I heard the bank president start to dial a phone number. I guess he was calling the bank's attorney."

About forty minutes later, Rick was back in the bank president's office with another member of the bank's staff . This time the bank president had something for Rick to proofread. It was an announcement for the local paper stating that due to ongoing labor disputes, Paradise Bank will take a neutral stance and will accept any good faith payments on loans carried by the involved parties until the dispute is settled. Thus the workers did not lose their homes or cars, Cheapskate finally provided health insurance as an employee benefit, and my leaflet is buried in the vast unknown labor history vault.

Of course, what I did was merely one day in the busy and hectic lives union employees live. As I was leaving Paradise, I put on my Bob Marley greatest hits CD. "Get Up Stand Up" was perfect to honor Rick's work. The workers will never know what Rick did for them and Cheapskate Factory hates him. Rick finished his story by saying, "If I ever had a problem with one of their products, I better use a pseudonym." Rick may not get respect, but he is doing what he feels is right. Solidarity!

ANDREW EVANS, JD, MLS, MAT is the Pickleball Librarian! He is a pickleball influencer and creator of the Pickleball Librarian Facebook page with over 14,000 dedicated followers. Andrew partners with pickleball brands providing hundreds of videos educating consumers on pickleball equipment, tips to improve play, advice on how to avoid injury and interviews top players dedicated to the sport as well as everyday rec players.

Andrew Evans, JD, MLS, MAT is the owner of Pickleball Librarian and Hokkien Martial Arts! He has also worked in the retail, legal, publishing, music, and library fields.

CATHY MARTIN, OIL ON CANVAS

Alone Together:
Chuck Warner

As the snow continued to fall on that January morning a few years back, I noticed how it muffled the traffic sounds on both 23rd and Massachusetts Streets. That peaceful stillness enabled me to hear the nostalgic low rumble and long mournful whistle of a distant locomotive passing through North Lawrence two miles away. The temperature hovered in the mid-teens; even the leaden sky seemed to shiver as the flakes slowly and softly fluttered to the ground. Rather than clear the accumulated snow from the driveway and sidewalk, I decided to just hunker down in my warm cozy home office until the snow stopped, supposedly later that afternoon.

I officially shared my home workplace with my wife Karen, but since she usually spent more of her time in her sewing room, the office always felt like my private place. Just large enough for our two desks and a few filing cabinets, it offered a snug but relaxed vibe. Incidentally, when the house was built, my office initially served as a second story sleeping porch on the back of our a hundred-year-old house on south Massachusetts Street. With three walls of oversized windows designed to let in summer evening breezes before air-conditioning, it commanded a spectacular 180-degree bird's eye view of my neighborhood. On that cold January morning, I gazed out my office window to a sea of snow-covered rooftops of early 20th century houses, all nestled under the branches of soaring eighty-foot oak trees. The view reminded me of my childhood treehouse where I spent hours alone with my thoughts. By the way, besides enjoying my panoramic view, my quiet and peaceful office has always been my favorite place for my post-retirement hobby, writing.

During my career I worked in business and banking, where my writing efforts were limited to memos, emails, and general correspondence, all of which were always functional, but not particularly interesting. However, several years after I retired, I began writing a book about the life of my maternal grandfather, a self-educated early pioneer at the University of Kansas Natural History Museum. When the idea to write that book was first suggested, I was skeptical and hesitant for two reasons. First, there was considerable self-doubt because I had never taken on a writing project as large as a book. Secondly, throughout my life I had never thought that I would enjoy writing because I always thought it a lonely endeavor considering how much time writers spend alone. Nevertheless, with time on my hands, I decided to give it a try.

As it turned out, I eventually wrote the book and even though I spent nearly ten years and thousands of hours all alone writing my book, in retrospect I never even once experienced loneliness. As it turned out, I really enjoyed writing because it allowed my imagination to go anywhere, which I found relaxing. Also, writing freed me to share feelings that I might not have otherwise. (That's where Karen says, "Duh!"). Also, much to my surprise, I found researching and organizing plot lines both intriguing and stimulating. Although the process was long and involved (writing, reading what you wrote, editing, reading again, reediting… rinse and repeat), I discovered being alone in my own thoughts very peaceful, especially when working from my familiar and comfy home office.

Even though I had not expected writing and my extended time of being alone to give me so much personal satisfaction, the bigger surprise was how well other writers seemed to get along and supported one another. As a banker, I was always cordial with my counterparts from other banks, but none of us seriously socialized with the competition. For instance, bankers would never have invited a banking competitor to join their regular golf group.

However, after I began writing, I discovered that writers were not like bankers. Although writers technically compete

THE
RAVEN
BOOK STORE
Lawrence, Kansas purveyors
of print on paper since 1987
www.ravenbookstore.com

against each other for publishers and readers, they all seemed to play well together. For instance, early on in my long journey of writing about my grandfather, on more than one occasion I asked experienced writers to read and comment on my work, which they did so willingly, and they always gave me helpful and constructive suggestions. I also learned that many writers join writing groups to read and critique each other's work, though I never could bring myself to do that since I never considered myself a "real" writer. After my book was published and received several awards, I felt confident enough as a writer to join a state-wide author's club and began to actually participate, including several readings. In the end, I always felt genuinely welcomed by other writers.

Comparing that experience to my time in banking, I wondered why writers behaved so differently. Is it because the acceptance by other writers stems from the understanding of what they have been through (all of the time alone with their words and ideas, the occasional self-doubt, and the pangs of vulnerability)? Is it a result of knowing and appreciating all the hard work invested in a final product? Or maybe they are just not as competitive as a bunch of bankers? Whatever the reason, I feel that the very act of writing seems to offer a kindred connection to this disparate group of writers, whose only common denominator might be that they enjoy their alone time.

Later that afternoon, when I noticed that the snow had stopped, I decided to leave my refuge and go wrestle the snow blower. Too bad some of my fellow writers didn't come over to help. I suppose they thought I like shoveling snow all alone.

CHUCK WARNER has lived in Lawrence since first attending the University of Kansas in the 1960s. With business and law degrees, he embarked on a nearly forty-year career in business and banking before retiring in 2008. After a 2009 family reunion and a behind the scenes tour of the KU Natural History Museum, he began exploring the idea of writing about his maternal grandfather and in 2019 *Birds,Bones, and Beetles: The Improbable Career and Remarkable Legacy of University of Kansas Naturalist Charles D. Bunker* was published by the University Press of Kansas. In 2020 his book was recognized as a Kansas Notable Book, won both the Martin Kansas History Book Award and the Looks Like a Million Book Award for best book layout from the Kansas Authors Club, and was a finalist in the High Plain Book Awards.

On Living Apart For A Time:
Julia Mathias Manglitz

Today marks the halfway point in a 111-day sojourn for work. An interlude that has me living part time in a city 1,100 miles and one-time zone away from home. In the last 56 days, I have spent five full days at home, eight traveling between the two cities, and 43 in my part-time home. My work has required extended and extensive travel before.

This time is different; I am away more weekends; I am flying, and I am much further from home. Last time, I learned that I needed to be kinder to myself.

I am effectively living alone. I feel a bit like I did when I went off to college. I have a studio apartment to myself with the bare necessities. And I have a larger, more comfortable, and familiar home where my family lives. In the apartment, I have upstairs neighbors whose lives run on a different schedule and tromp on the floor in ways that sound alarming down here. It's likely just the result of typical daily tasks, I remind myself.

I miss the quiet of the country at home where our modest old farmhouse, small by Midwest standards, sits peacefully separated from our neighbors by acres of pastures, a creek, and tree lines. I can play music and sing along loudly without fear of offending anyone but my husband and pets, who will forgive me. I miss my husband and our beloved trio of pets: two rambunctious cats and our goofy, oversized, aging dog.

My husband and I are both introverts—we need our time alone. Sometimes, for one of us to be genuinely alone, the other must leave the house or at least go outside for a while. Perhaps our natures make being alone and apart easier for both of us. On the other hand, perhaps not, because each of us has a tiny trove of trusted confidants outside of each other.

I've done things solo a lot in my life. I first flew a plane solo when I was 17. It was terrifying and exhilarating. I can still summon the lightheaded, giddy, weak-in-the-knees feeling I had after landing and getting out of the plane, even though it was nearly 40 years ago. I have driven back and forth across Missouri alone so many times since I was 17 that I can't count them anymore. I was in my 30s before everyone had a cell phone. When I was a teenager, my father would put his portable CB radio in my car and attach the giant magnetic antenna on top of the roof with a clunk – "just in case," he would say.

It occurs to me that this is the most he's been on his own and the most I've been alone in a long time. I have relearned how to shop and cook for one. He has learned how little salt I put in our food because now he eats out and brings home leftovers to save him from cooking—a return to bachelor ways.

As a Gen-Xer, I was one of a generation encouraged to get out of the house and wander as far as we could on foot or our bikes, so long as we were home by dark. Our parents taught us about stranger danger, but in our middle-class neighborhoods, most women stayed home; there was always a house where an adult could be summoned if needed. We grew up in a world with ample opportunity to test and develop our judgment with a safety net.

I've done things solo a lot in my life. I first flew a plane solo when I was 17. It was terrifying and exhilarating. I can still summon the light-headed, giddy, weak-in-the-knees feeling I had after landing and getting out of the plane, even though it was nearly 40 years ago. I have driven back and forth across Missouri alone so many times since I was 17 that I can't count them anymore. I was in my 30s before everyone had a cell phone. When I was a teenager, my father would put his portable CB radio in my car and attach the giant magnetic antenna on top of the roof with a clunk—"just in case," he would say. In retrospect, I don't know what my parents were thinking. I looked older than my 17 years, and I was driving a black sports car—the things that men said to me and about me over that radio were frequently obscene. Perhaps it was good that I knew how to drive that car to its limits; a couple of times, my willingness to shatter the speed limit probably saved my skin.

I've traveled solo for work—countless driving and flying trips to Oklahoma, Texas, and western Kansas. I went to Italy alone on a business trip in 2017. A couple of ladies traveling together sat across the aisle from me, and we struck up a conversation. They were maybe ten years older than me. That I would make such a journey solo dumbfounded them. I explained that I would meet others when I arrived in Vernona and that it was not my first overseas or foreign travel. But they could not fathom traveling, save to the grocery store, alone. I still wonder if society changed that much between the Boomers and Gen-X or whether I'm as odd as they seemed to think me.

This sojourn for work is only possible because of my husband. There is no way I could bring all three of our beloved pets to this tiny apartment. It would be torture for them, not to mention the neighbors. If we had children, I don't think I could do this at all. The guilt of being away would be more than I could bear. I feel guilty enough leaving a grown man and three pets alone together.

The work I am here to do is amazing; it is truly a once-in-a-lifetime chance for me. And as I'm getting closer to the end of my career than the beginning, the urgency of grasping those opportunities becomes more poignant. I am fortunate to have a partner who accepts this deep-seated drive of mine, a drive that I don't fully understand; I don't know where it comes from. It contradicts my desire to be home, to be grounded, to be safe, to be quiet and still. I can't reconcile the two sides of nature; my husband says there is nothing to reconcile, only to accept.

I have many solitary hours to myself. Weekends here

are difficult. I go to museums and attractions, and being alone in a crowd is usually distracting and comforting. But sometimes, I see something my husband would love, and I am overcome. He is not there to share the experience. This pain is not unfamiliar; it goes back to the summer I studied abroad. The day I visited the Uffizi Gallery in Florence and beheld Michelangelo's "David," I grieved because my mother, an artist who so admired his work, was not there. I broke down and cried. She had encouraged me to return to school for architecture; I would not have been in Florence otherwise. She had nursed me through my fears of going abroad and enabled this trip by taking in my dog and cat for the summer. She deserved to see this exquisite work of art with her own eyes; I did not feel worthy. My mother passed away 20 years ago; I contend with this feeling nearly every time I see an exceptional work of art anywhere. But feeling this way about my husband is fresh.

Last weekend, I stopped in a park. I got some lunch from a kiosk and sat to eat, contemplate my adventures, and write a little. I looked up when I heard a child nearby giggling. She was dressed in a floral printed bucket hat and overalls, twirling in circles with a stuffed panda bear. She hugged and kissed the bear and twirled some more. No other adults were nearby—she was utterly alone in her world with her bear. Her joy infected me; I could not help smiling and quietly laughing. Then panic struck me. Where were her parents? It took me some minutes of looking around to find them. They were watching from a safe distance, but a surprisingly long distance for a small child in such a large, open public place—at least in this day of helicopter parents. As I calmed down, I returned to the joy of watching her inhabit her world of make believe. It was on unabashed display for anyone who cared to notice.

Like a child, I go to bed early. I call home every night, usually just before I go to sleep. It is the most lonesome time for me. I miss cuddling with my pets at bedtime, but most of all, I miss spooning with my husband. We dated off and on for thirteen years and have been married now for twenty. We were slow to commit and married later in life. Falling asleep cuddled with him has been a comfort and a mainstay for most of my adult life. Our nightly phone conversations include a run-down of our respective days. Sometimes, the call is short, sometimes long. Sometimes we watch a TV show together— I call those our "When Harry Met Sally" moments, like when they watch "Casablanca" together while talking on the phone. Our calls always end with "I miss you," "I love you," and "Good night, sweetheart."

When I come home, the hugs last longer, the kisses are sweeter and more lingering. The time apart seems to have indeed made our hearts grow fonder—or revert to a former fondness that years of familiarity had dulled. In this milestone year of our marriage, it seems to have reminded us to savor the time we have, to cherish each other and the life we have worked hard to build. His mother is the only parent we still have with us after twenty years of marriage. My father passed away just this year. We are both keenly aware that someday, one of us will be left without the other; it is not for us to know the when, where, or how of it. But we know the day will come. Neither of us wants to be the one left behind, and neither of us wants to be the one to leave the other. This time that I am away for work is part preparation for that day and part reminder to live our life together on our own terms and for our own sake.

JULIA MATHIAS MANGLITZ is a seasoned preservation architect with over 20 years of experience helping clients maintain and update their historical structures. She grew up all over the Midwest and has chosen to settle in rural Douglas County, Kansas, with her husband and an evolving menagerie of pets; the current incarnation consists of two precocious cats and a goofy dog. Julia finds joy and beauty equally in the natural and built environments. Since childhood, old buildings and the stories they tell captivated her imagination as much as any well-told tale. Beyond her architectural endeavours, Julia channels her creativity into writing short stories and chronicling her life experience in personal essays.

Parkland:
Robert Fraga

Excerpted From *A Parade Of Grief, 2024*

On the Valentine's Day massacre, young Hogg had the presence of mind to turn on his cell phone's video recorder to narrate events as they unfolded. Alone in his car afterward, David Hogg began screaming, "Fuck!" He began smashing his fists on the dashboard. Then he sent his video to a local newspaper where he worked as an intern. His career as a media star was launched.

Biking back to school the day of the shooting, David was interviewed by Laura Ingraham of *FOX News*. He told her, "I don't want this to be just another mass shooting; I don't want this to be something that people forget."

Six a.m. the following morning he was prepping for an interview with George Stephanopoulos of MSNBC.

The Twitter followings of both David Hogg and Emma Gonzalez soared. As was to be expected, there was a glut of hostility directed particularly against Hogg, who was more acerbic and assertive than Gonzalez. The young man was accused, of course, of being a crisis actor. Death threats poured in. His mother received a note which said, "Fuck with the NRA and you'll be DOA." At the rally in Washington, D.C., Hogg called for a boycott of Laura Ingraham who had accused him of whining because he hadn't been admitted to UCLA. Ingraham later apologized for this slur after a sizeable number of her sponsors—companies like Johnson & Johnson, Nestlé, Jenny Craig and Ruby Tuesday—dropped out. "I'm glad to see corporate America standing with me and the other students of Parkland," Hogg commented. "When we work together, we can accomplish anything." As things worked out, Hogg was admitted to Harvard. UCLA's loss, it turned out, was Harvard's gain. Hogg planned to go to Harvard and study political science there. Emma Gonzalez was accepted at New College, a prestigious liberal arts school in Sarasota, Florida, and she planned to go there and room with her best friend from Douglas High.

March for Our Lives became a fixture in the gun control firmament, long out-living the actual march on Washington which had spawned the movement. *Buzzfeed News* reported that the incorporation of three young Black students onto its board effectively integrated what had previously been a lily-white group. One of the new board members, Bria Smith, 18, from Milwaukee voiced her objection to the exclusivity of the MFOL leadership this way: "There's a bunch of White kids getting millions of dollars …I'm like, what about Black Lives Matter? What about my cousin who was shot and killed and there was no justice for him?"

HuffPost, quoting a PR firm handling press requests for the campaign, reported that a number of celebrities had made hefty contributions. These included Oprah Winfrey, George and Amal Clooney and Gucci, all of whom had ponied up half a million dollars to MFOL. Some of the adults assisting the Parkland students with their finances were well known. These included the chair of the Board of Regents of the University of California and a member of the (Quaker) Friends Committee on National Legislation.

The summer of 2018 Gonzalez and Hogg organized a nation-wide tour to register young voters. It actually registered 50,000. The bus carried between eighteen and twenty-two students as well as one therapist and three security guards. It hit seventy-five cities in two months. One of those cities was Huntington Beach, California. There, David Hogg led a march from the rallying grounds where he shouted out, "Tell me what democracy looks like!"

The bus tour opened the students' eyes to a world radically different from their own. David Hogg, for example, lived in a gated community in Parkland, Florida. On the tour, he encountered the father of Michael Brown. Hogg remembered that meeting this way:

He told us to close our eyes and imagine the person that we love most, that we hold dearest. And then imagine them being shot and left on hot asphalt for four hours. And not knowing where they were, if that was them, and not being able to see them. I imagined my sister. I imagined Emma. I was really just thinking of, like, pretty much everybody on our team, because we're all family now.

The Parkland students were shadowed on part of their tour of the country by a group which called itself the Utah Gun Exchange. That group fancied itself on a "freedom tour." It rode around in a vehicle described by *The New York Times* as "a tank with a machine-gun turret." It is not known whether any body of protestors, like the Utah Gun Exchange, called what the Parkland students were doing a Children's Crusade.

An example of the static which David Hogg provoked on NRATV: It came from that channel's commentator, Colion Noir. Noir—a stage name; his birth name was Collins Iyare Idehen, Jr.—is a gun rights enthusiast. He began raging against Hogg for saying that he was fighting for helpless Black people.

Who the hell gave @davidhogg111 the authority to put on his White man's burden costume to save me from myself by marching to restrict my right to own a gun that at one point I wasn't considered human enough to own? That is the shit we're cosigning?

There were, of course, positive reactions to the Parkland students' odyssey. Chief among these was a handwritten letter from Barack and Michelle Obama sent only days before the March for Our Lives.

"We wanted to let you know how inspired we have been by the resilience, resolve and solidarity that you have all shown in the wake of unspeakable tragedy," the letter said. "Not only have you supported and comforted each other, you've helped awaken the conscience of the nation."

Throughout our history, young people like you have led the way in making America better [the letter went on]. There may be setbacks, you may feel like progress is too slow in coming. But we have no doubt that you are going to make an enormous difference in the days and years to come.

In the fall of 2018, days before the midterm elections, an op-ed piece coauthored by Hogg and Gonzalez appeared in the *Washington Post.* They commented on their recent cross-country tour which took them to conservative regions like Bismarck, ND where "the mayor and state representative arrived at our town hall meeting to head a counter-rally right outside." They further wrote:

> Other times, people have shown up at our events armed to the teeth [they wrote] shouting our names and accusing us of being `crisis actors.' We've gone out to meet them. We've explained that we're not the gun-grabbing communists they think we are—that when people advocated for safer roads and cars, they weren't anti-vehicle. We're trying to keep people from dying. Sometimes, the people we talk to end up in tears. Usually we end up finding common ground.

The Parkland students wielded influence world-wide. They inspired among others a young autistic Swedish girl, Greta Thunberg, who became an environmental superstar. Her activism gained—and retained—the world's unflagging admiration.

What does the future hold for David Hogg? He has told reporters that, after canvasing for candidates he supported, he would attend college where he planned to read a "shitload of books."

When he turns 25, Hogg plans to run for Congress.

ROBERT FRAGA grew up in Los Alamos, New Mexico, where his father helped make the atomic bomb and where Bob worked in the Los Alamos National Laboratory during summer vacations while at at Pomona College. Bob then moved to Canada. After graduating with his PhD at the University of British Columbia (1963-65), he moved to the Middle East, where he lived the next twenty years. He taught at the American University in Cairo where he learned a smattering of Arabic. Bob wrote *The Greening of Oz* (2012), about the town of Greensburg in western Kansas, that "came back green" after a tornado almost wiped it out, and in 2020, *The Road through San Judas* (2020), about the struggle between landless farmers and the wealthy Mexican family who wanted them gone. Bob lives in Lawrence, Kansas, and spends his summers in a 15th century home in rural France.

Noticing Solitude And Sanctuary:
Gretchen Cassel Eick

Outside my study the red maple tree fills the wall of windows that face the back yard. Its branches splay from the trunk soaring up, its fingered leaves shimmer, a vibrant, verdant canvas in the sunlight. Squirrels play tag along its arms.

I see it through my window and thank whoever planted it there.

I have not always noticed. Then one spring day when the tree was deep pink, I did notice. Noticing changed my life.

Its branches were covered in rose-colored knots. Leaves waiting to uncurl. An overture in pink.

I stopped working on lesson plans, stopped assuming my days would follow the familiar pattern they had for twenty years.

Why haven't I noticed?

Thirty minutes later when my spouse entered my study I pointed to the tree beyond the windows. "I'm retiring," I said with conviction.

"It's only four in the afternoon."

"I mean retiring from the university. I need to notice the beauty around me."

When the leaves opened and filled the air outside my window with small green waving hands, I noticed. And I began to write. I wrote that autumn as I watched them transition to scarlet and crimson, and when they let go and dropped to meet the ground. I wrote while my maple became a skeleton, a maze of sharp-angled tree-bones dividing the sky like leaded glass into myriad patches of blue and white and gray.

I did not return to the university. Most mornings I walked along the river before sitting down at my window to write. I noticed the river's contradictions, so like my own…how wind tugged its surface skin north while the current pulled its dark interior south. That felt familiar and I noticed.

Six books later, sitting at my desk, I remembered. I was eight and sitting with my father and brother on the New Jersey seashore. Dad's father had recently died and his wife — our mother — had left us. He bent over a small spiral notebook writing with a stubby pencil in his unintelligible scrawl.

I worried about him, wishing I was big enough to take care of him.

"What are you writing, Daddy?" I asked.

"A hymn." His smile was gentle and inviting. "Want to hear it?" He sang in his rich baritone, holding back his volume so as not to disturb the other sunbathers. He sang about the ocean and the sky and the sun stirring him, teaching him that we are not alone.

"This is thy world, O Lord,
This is thy world.
The ocean waves
thy glorious flag unfurled
Proclaiming thee
Eternally
The mighty sea
Waves out thy victory.

The sun is thine, O Lord,
The sun is thine.
It makes the body warm
And stirs the mind
That we might grow
Under its glow
Until we know
That we are yours also.

The sky is blue, O Lord,
The sky is blue

The heavens declare your works
And we would too.
Through all our days
In all our ways
We sing our praise
To you always."

Amidst the disruption of his life and anxiety about the future he noticed the natural world around him. It reminded him that he was part of an age-old chorus whose praise-singing stretched across eons, witnessing to the presence of the Holy, even in the worst of times.

Many decades removed from that moment, I send Dad my thanks for his life lesson, grateful I now notice.

Visiting and living in other countries shapes Gretchen's life. She taught in Latvia and Bosnia and Herzegovina and worked for 14 years as a foreign policy lobbyist. She wrote two award-winning scholarly histories and five novels (the latest, Dark Crossings, 2022). She was Kansas Authors Club's Prose Writer of 2021.

HEATHER DURIS, WHAT I LEAVE BEHIND

PART II:
POETRY

Poems submitted for the Winter 2023/2024 edition of *The Write Bridge* include considering shadows, fleeing across space and time, what you've left behind, what he's left behind and what's been eclipsed. Wisdom is offered from the old birds of the forest, and from friends gathered on game night at Sully's bar, and more.

BARBARA WATERMAN PETERS, MWS: THE MESSENGERS

BARBARA WATERMAN-PETERS, (BFA, Washburn University, MFA, Kansas State University, Honorary Doctor of Fine Arts, Washburn University) taught at Washburn and Kansas State Universities as well as for Lassen Community College in California. She has received a Certificate of Recognition for Outstanding Achievement from the State of Kansas and the Monroe Award from the Washburn University Alumni Association. In 2011 she was awarded the ARTY for Distinguished Visual Artist from ARTS Connect in Topeka. Her work has been included in more than 300 solo, group and juried exhibits. She is represented by several galleries, Jones in Kansas City, SNW in Manhattan, and Beauchamp in Topeka. She owns STUDIO 831 in the North Topeka Arts & Entertainment District (NOTO).

Shadow Questions:
Barbara Waterman Peters

Have you considered shadows,
Truly looked when you're alone?
Not as metaphor or time trace,
But as phenomena
Present.

Have you wondered about shape,
Size, color, direction?
Not as objects or chance
But as shapeshifters
Flowing.

Do you note shimmering wisps,
Chimera, dancers?
Not as beings following,
But leading, embracing,
Subtle.

Do you observe the movements,
Translucent, magic?
Not as confined or tied to you,
But as independent,
Changing.

Will you consider shadows,
Soft, crisp, dark, or pale?
Not as unavoidable fact,
But as gifts, giving a
Light show.

WORDS LEFT UNSPOKEN

J.A. McGovern

Discover life's untold stories through J.A. McGovern's evocative poetry. Walk city streets, bask in meadows, and journey through spirituality, love, and adventure in _Words Left Unspoken_.

Finalist: Amity Literary Prize, 2023

JEWELRY BY JULIE

Handmade Jewelry By Julie Kingsbury

17 W. 9th St | Lawrence, KS 66044

_(785) 434-5154_

You:
J.A. McGovern

Between a short faded death
Lie two lights
One - the gift of contentment
Other - the gift of sorrow

And today I saw the final night of my life
Between long somber breaths, lie two codes
One - the symbol of song
Other - the symbol of poem

A song - I chanted hallelujah in the streams
I looked to the east
Wandering the desert with broken feet
Only to find a content heart never to succeed

A poem - what I saw I never knew
A soul instilled by two
Passion and sorrow - the night turned blue
Inside my heart I knew it was you

Tonight will be the final night, followed by my last day
Tomorrow will be somber, life taken away
But tonight will remain enriched
Contentment and I blue, thinking of you

J.A. MCGOVERN is a published poet, songwriter, and independent filmmaker. A graduate, with a bachelor's degree in forensic science—chemistry focus with criminal justice minor, J.A. McGovern currently works as an analytical inorganic chemist. Founder and curator of the literary art anthology *Perception* his artistic team has received multiple nominations and awards for their work. In 2018, J.A. McGovern received an American Songwriting Award for lyrics in folk music, for his independent film's title song, *All Over Again*. *Words Left Unspoken* is J.A. McGovern's first poetry collection publication.

An American Looks at
Su Shi's *Night*:
Portrayed in Qiao Zhongchang's "Illustration to the Second Prose Poem on the Red Cliff"
Vern Barnet

You left your friends to be alone,
unsettled into nature's rocks and streams,
familiar trees were changed as moonlight shown
into mystery and history's regimes.
The overgrowth and tangles trip your voice
to shout into the cliff which echoes out
a question charged, Do we have fate or choice?
With crane's sharp cry your quiet boat marks doubt.

I see you dream Immortals in your home,
but what is space and time and really real?
How much environment, how much genome?
Are choices freely made or by fate's wheel?

So Han, or Gettysburg, or World Trade plots—
In God's great gambling house, are such just slots?

A Note About The Poem:
Qiao Zhongchang was active in the early 12th Century. The handscroll inspiring this sonnet was itself inspired by the earlier poem by Su Shi (late 11th Century). This world-famous work is in the collection of the Nelson-Atkins Museum of Art in Kansas City, MO.

For eighteen years VERN BARNET wrote the weekly *Faiths and Beliefs* column for The Kansas City Star. His book of 154 sonnets, *Thanks for Noticing: The Interpretation of Desire*, was published in 2015 (La Vita Nuova press). He was developmental editor for *Binding Us Together: A Civil Rights Activist Reflects on a Lifetime of Community and Public Service* by Alvin Brooks (Andrews McMeel, 2021). He has taught at several seminaries and is Minister Emeritus at the Center for Religious Experience and Study.

Untitled:
Anamarie Davis-Wilkins

I ran in the direction
Of the sun,
Heart racing
Fast feet moving,
Escaping the darkness
Behind me.

My mind racing with me,
It too taking
The jarring leaps of the
Explained, unexplained
Complicated reasons.

I took flight that day,
Fleeing across space and time,
Only to suddenly slam
Into a mirrored image of myself.

ANAMARIE DAVIS-WILKINS is a Mom, proud grandmother, birth doula, writer and poet. She has enjoyed reading and writing since childhood. Her first book of poems is *Reminiscence,* and her first novel is *Under and Over.* Recently, she had a piece published by Poet Laureate of Kansas. She has work published in numerous anthologies and online magazines. She is an active participant in Speak Easy Poets of Topeka, Sunflower Poetry Society of Kansas, and the National Federation of State Poetry Societies.

"Much in the style of the sweeping works of Cormac McCarthy or Ian McEwan, we take a philosophical look at American values and the struggle of what it is to be American via Gurley's epic story. ...Gurley delivers an intricate, character-based portrayal of two very specific men and their conflicts, struggles, fall from grace, and attempts to claw their lives back together, but on the wider plane, there's an important message about the heavy price of progress brewing in the modern world. What results is an exceedingly well-penned, dramatic slow-burner of a tale that will have you truly gripped and deep in thought by its conclusion. ... highly recommend." — *Reviewed By K.C. Finn for Readers' Favorite*

"George Gurley has the eye and ear of a poet. His descriptions of the weather, the landscape, the wild animals set the stage for the adversities and aspirations of the prairie state." — *Playwright Frank Higgins, "The Sweet By 'n' By," "Black Pearl Sings."*

"The novel's inciting conflicts—between personal histories, rare and teeming ecologies, and commercial progress—are fascinating." —*Karen Rigby, Foreword Reviews*

"This is a spendid story set in the American Midwest" —*David Garrard Lowe, author "Lost Chicago"*

What You've Left Behind:
George Gurley

I found a frozen bird,
its eyes eaten as if they'd seen too much.
It made me think I didn't want to know
where that car of yours has dragged its mufflers.
I found boxes of botany texts in the garage
and wondered what you saved,
what you took away when you skipped
and why you left that bird behind.

You keep leaving, like the scoured snow in Antarctica
that changes into vapor by sublimation
without first melting.
Some are torn from flight
by a microburst called windshear.
Some keep picking up the pieces,
trying to teach the no-shows
and the dead beats about keeping promises.

I've rehearsed alibis for you
and become addicted to placebos,
the more I taste your hoped-for makeup kiss.
Maybe my mistake was thinking of you as a tenant
and that I had a lease on you.
I suppose we all keep giving up
and leaving our books and homes,
imagining the neighbors are blindfolded
and can't watch us sneak away,
dreaming of a new life,
leaving what we know behind.
And the landlords are always left
holding the bag,
figuring up their losses,
telling anyone who'll listen:
I'll never see them again.

What He Left Behind:
Brian Daldorph

A sister who says: "He'd been dead to me a long time."

A small yellow house by Mule Creek
with overgrown yard and roof needing repair.

A few students who'd liked his classes
though they don't remember too much about them.

Fifteen chapters of his novel, untitled.

Two boxes full of dusty CDs.

Three photograph albums
and a plastic bag full of loose photographs.

A flat-screen TV, two tables,
an armchair with ripped armrest,
two plastic picnic chairs.

Four pairs of running shoes, new to old.

His painting of a sunset over a river.

Three notebooks full of microscopic writing.

The small stink of loneliness.

BRIAN DALDORPH teaches at the University of Kansas and Douglas County Jail. He edits Coal City Review. His most recent books of poetry are Ice Age/ Edad de Hielo (Irrupciones P, 2017), Blue Notes (Dionysia P, 2019), and Kansas Poems (Meadowlark P, 2021).

Eclipse:
Bruce Rolfe

Moon shadow drifting
Silent as owl's feathered wings,
Blotting out the sun.

BRUCE ROLFE, a former U.S. Navy Search & Rescue pilot for 20 years, is proud to say there are nine souls here today because he was there then. He is the author of the Chip Hale handyman series of mystery novels, *Tools of the Trade, Trademark of Murder*, and *Trade Secrets*. His next book, *Family Trade* is forthcoming. Bruce also has a new standalone book coming out from Dingbat Publishing. *The Little Storehouse in the Middle of the Block* is the memoir of a wannabe writer, who at 47, discovered after his mother's death that he was adopted, she was murdered, and his quest to find his biological parents. Find Bruce here: http://brucerolfe.com/

Murder at the Arlington

By Kathleen Kaska

In the shadows of 1952, reporter Sydney Lockhart checks into the historic Arlington Hotel in Hot Springs, Arkansas. Before she unpacks, she discovers the brutally murdered body of the hotel's bookkeeper. What began as a simple travel-writing assignment turns into a murder investigation with Sydney as a suspect.

Determined to clear her name and prove herself a reporter deserving more than travel assignments, Sydney becomes embroiled in the underworld of gangsters and gamblers. In her fight for the truth, she faces a more urgent battle-saving her own skin. She also meets a handsome police detective who's unconvinced of her innocence. Can Sydney solve the crime before she's arrested? Find out in the first book in the Sydney Lockhart Mystery series, Murder at the Arlington.

Alone on the Wing:
Kathleen Kaska

Alone on a frosty morning too cold for comfort

I stand in an open field,
the steam from my silver coffee mug
rises up to warm my face.
A deep orange color lightens the sky,
Announcing the sunrise.
I was the first to arrive, now
dozens of others quietly mill around,
for the moment is too precious for idle chat.
An hour later, most have given up,
retreated to the warmth of their cars.
My eyes burn cold with tears.
I focus on the northwestern sky.
My cup has cooled, but I stay put.
I've waited too long for this moment.
A radio crackles and a soft voice reports
our guests are just beyond the ridge,
slowed by a stiff headwind.
My throat constricts and I see a white V-shape
appear against the now bluing sky.

And off the ultralight's left wing
a linear trail of ten small Vees.
Ten young whooping cranes on their first migration.

My tears now flow and warm my face with joy.

KATHLEEN KASKA writes the award-winning mystery series the Sydney Lockhart Mystery Series set in the 1950s. Her first two Sydney Lockhart mysteries were bonus books for the Pulpwood Queen Book Group, the country's largest book group. She also writes mystery trivia, including *The Sherlock Holmes Quiz Book*. Her short story, *The Adventure at Old Basingstoke*, appears in *Sherlock Holmes of Baking Street*. She founded The Dogs in the Nighttime and the Sherlock Holmes Society of Anacortes. Her latest Sydney Lockhart mystery, *Murder at the Pontchartrain*, has just been released.

Sound of Solitude:
Kelly W. Johnston

The south breeze through the grass and trees
is the dominant sound at sundown. A few
chorus frogs start giggling, then quiet.
An errant waft lifts the edge of my paper.
I stop writing and watch.

No rabbits appear to steal birdseed. No crows
announce an evening patrol. No bobwhites call
to covey. No coyotes yip or howl. No geese churn
the lake surface with feet and wings as they leave.
Even the crickets are strangely silent.

On the inflamed horizon, a jet contrail escapes.
The turbine atop the storm shelter slowly spins,
scraping against weeds that hide it from the wind.
A couple of birds are peeping in the hedgerow. Are
they discussing the seed I scattered, cautious
about leaving the safety of cedar branches?

As the harvest moon climbs above the treeline,
a Great Horned Owl issues a one-note warning,
then repeats. A whippoorwill begins an incessant
greeting to the descending darkness. A thud
is heard in the treeline as a hedge apple
crashes to earth. Another contrail rises
and merges with the Milky Way.

KELLY JOHNSTON is a life-long Kansan who graduated from Wichita State University in 1977 while majoring in creative writing. He studied under A. G. Sobin, Anita Skeen and L. M. Grow. While at WSU, he published poems in *Mikrokosmos*, *The Cottonwood Review* and the *Ark River Review*. More recently, he has published poems in the *California Quarterly* (Vol. 43, #3), *The Flint Hills Review* and the *I-70 Review*. His chapbooks *Kalaska* (2017) and *Tumbleweed* (2021) were both published by the Blue Cedar Press. Kelly loves to spend time on his land in the Chautauqua Hills near Cross Timbers State Park where most of his poems have been inspired.

Watkins Park
Patricia Cleveland

Walk the silent trails of Watkins Park and
You will see the old birds of the forest
High up in the trees in their cage of wire and wood
They no longer try to fly
They just sit and stare into the sky above
The canopy that shades their eyes

What did they see before…

A raptor knows what's good to eat
And what to leave alone
He can hear the mouse beneath the leaves
Or a cricket on the run
He doesn't know about the poison pill or the gun
Or the metaphor that's come undone

Like us…

If you set them free they won't survive
The light's gone out behind their eyes
But what, what are they doing there?
They're sitting there for you and me
So we can see what used to be
When people used to care.

Kibbles and bits for the lords of the air…

Luna One:
Duane L. Herrmann

"Working this dozer
in this suit,
such a crap job,
almost done!
Construction can start
on the base of the dome
to seal this crater
then we can start
making air!" Jaxon thought,
as he stared out
into black space,
huts and equipment
huddled
inside the crater below
waiting
to be shielded from space
so life could begin
on the moon.

DUANE L. HERRMANN, a reluctant carbon-based life-form, was surprised to find himself in 1951 on a farm in Kansas. He's still trying to make sense of it but has grown fond of grass waving under wind, trees and moonlight. He aspires to be a hermit, but would miss his children, grandchildren and a few friends. He is known to carry baby kittens in his mouth, pet snakes, and converse with owls, but is careful not to anger them! His full-length collections of poetry include: *Prairies of Possibilities, Ichnographical:173, Family Plowing, Remnants of a Life, No Known Address, Praise the King of Glory* and *Gedichte aus Prairies of Possibilities*, plus a science fiction novel, and a number of chapbooks. Individual work has been published in more than a dozen anthologies and *Midwest Quarterly, Little Balkans Review, Flint Hills Review, Orison, Inscape, Lily Literary Journal, Hawai'i Review* and others in print and online in English and other languages he can't read. He is the recipient of the Robert Hayden Poetry Fellowship 1989, and the Ferguson Kansas History Book Award 2007. He survived a traumatic, abusive childhood embellished with dyslexia, ADHD (both unknown at the time), cyclothymia, situational mutism, an anxiety disorder, and PTSD.

Unlock the self through verse. Ian Cook's poetic odyssey traces silence to speech, forging connection through language, sound, and symbols. A journey of growth, mental health, and resonating authenticity.

"Vishuddha is the Sanskrit name for the fifth chakra (or focal point, used in meditation),   located in the throat.   It is related to communication, self-expression, creativity and personal truth, all of which I found in Ian Cook's first book of poems. .... if you're prepared to go on the journey with the poet as your guide, you will learn plenty, including new ways of seeing and experiencing the world." —*Brian Daldorph, editor of Coal City Review. His most recent books of poetry are Ice Age/Edad de Hielo (Irrupciones P, 2017), Blue Notes (Dionysia P, 2019), and Kansas Poems (Meadowlark P, 2021).*

"I suggest that you do not hasten through the pages of this collection." —*Alaya Mira Anonda*

Cook's new book is penned with the intimate gentle candor of diary entries, but with the universal touch and appeal of a Whitman poem. ... cosmic ... savory, but sweet." —*Kevin Rabas, More Than Words, Past Poet Laureate of Kansas*

Cook brings together the Kansas prairie and family, solitude and unusual communion in this divining collection. Vishudda is a gem from a multi-talented artist and poet." — *Chloe Seim, Author of Churn, Winner of the 2022 George Garrett Fiction Prize*

L'appel Du Vide
Ian Cook

I lit a cigarette at the wrong end and smoked it halfway
stubbed   dead   ash   upon   palms
to smear long letters on a wall
unafraid of wayward winds and letting go, of change
tending noticed glances and half smiles, set loose
made sure they were counted for
board up in the whole silence of sacred solitude
nourished, licking fingers slogged with ink
spitting up unhurried cursive in the exhale
in the frail consciousness of waking breath
the length of the larynx distends
the wind bending the sigh
exhaling a ghost
still husk

when I die I'll be closer to god because I won't   exist

At his core, IAN COOK is a mutt. An amalgamation of many things—different races, Swedish/German patronage, Chinese-Indonesian matronage, raised internationally. An in-between, a hybrid being, flowing, swimming, a life in and out of water, amphibious. He is a collection of multitudes, many selves, many-masks, anxiety, depression, bipolar disorder, sleeplessness, and dreams that don't end. He receives waves, whispers, and frequencies from beyond and translates them into Art, Music, and Poetry. Ian Cook is the author of Vishuddha, a collection of poetry that deals with communication, what it is, and how the individual does it: by speaking, singing, screaming, writing, drawing, expressing, playing, by communing with All. He has had work featured in online and print journals such as *Snarl Journal*, KU's *Kiosk Magazine*, *Avatar Review*, and others. Ian lives, writes, draws, sings, and plays in Lawrence, Kansas, with his partner Maddie, pups Mildred, and Cordelia, and rats Remy, and Grandpa.

Pandemic Sketch - Alone:
Lindsey Bartlett

Over a year into the pandemic,
I have forgotten how to enjoy
being alone. Instead, the anxiety
increases each day:
heart beats rapid,
stomach churning,
my thoughts spinning in circles.
I long for human companionship
in ways I never did pre-pandemic.
Jealous, for the first time, of those with
spouses or kids, while it is just me battling
this time of isolation.
I used to pride myself on how unbothered I was
to do so much alone, but pride go'eth before a fall.
So, I scroll the contacts in my phone, looking for that one
person who might answer, provide a companionship
yet unfound.

LINSDEY BARTLETT teaches composition and literature at Emporia State University. Bartlett's poetry can be found in her book, *Vacant Childhood*. Additional writings and photography have appeared in *The Milk House: A Rural Writing Collective*, *The Write Bridge*, *Flint Hills Review*, and *105 Meadowlark Reader*.

The Last Two Minutes:
Mark Scheel

I awaken from a dream of a strange place
with strange people I don't know.
The day is cloudy. No sun rays to greet me.
There's a February chill in the air.

Last night at Sully's bar I watched
the KU/Texas game—on the big screen,
with Bob. I only see him on game nights.
I don't even know where he lives.
He never reads my poems.

KU was leading most of the second half,
but Texas, as they say, still hung in.
As the clock wound down, **Texas** made a run,
but KU held the lead. Then, in the last two minutes,
Dick hit two three-pointers, and stretched it to twelve.

In those last two minutes, the victory was sealed.
I could breathe easy. High-five Bob. Laugh again.

This morning, assembling my work-to-do list,
knowing that wind outside would likely hold an edge,
I wished I was back at Sully's. Last night.
For those last two minutes.
When life was simply a ball through a net—
and strangers all cheering together.

MARK SCHEEL has served overseas with the American Red Cross, taught at Emporia State University, was a public library information specialist and helped edit *Kansas City Voices* magazine. He co-authored the book *Of Youth and the River* and his collection of stories and poems, *A Backward View*, was awarded the 1998 J. Donald Coffin Memorial Book Award from the Kansas Authors Club. More recent works include the blog collection The Pebble: Life, Love, Politics and Geezer Wisdom, the fiction collection *And Eve Said Yes*, the poetry collection *Star Chaser* and the novel *The Potter's Wheel*.

Laundry Day:
John Ritchie

I pick through the basket
reading underwear
like tea leaves.
She sometimes wears
her public face at home,
leaving her laundry to ask
for the help she could not.
A bad week:
just two sets of underwear.
My own conscience soiled.
Had I noticed?
What else had I ignored?
But it's been awhile since those times.
Better.
The basket still speaks.
7 pairs for 7 days.
Soft comforts
in a basket
of clean laundry.

JOHN RITCHIE has been a Kansas educator for 24 years. He currently teaches English for juniors, seniors, and Washburn University students in Topeka. When he is not sharing his passion for reading and writing with his students, he is reminding himself to engage in his own writing for pleasure and tell the stories that are bubbling away inside. He enjoys plowing through his endless to-be-read list, walking Topeka's Shunga trail, and trying to raise vegetables in his backyard garden. He lives in Topeka with his wife and two cats.

Friendship Fountain:
Peg Nichols

I dream alone.
I dream in solitude.
I dream of a fountain,
A friendship fountain
To be presented as a heartfelt gift
For the brave people of Ukraine.

I need an engineer.
I need a hydraulics engineer.
I need an experienced hydraulics engineer.
To bend the pipes, install the pumps,
Design the valves and the weirs.
Now I am not alone, two together, not alone.

We search some sculptors.
We search a few skilled sculptors
To craft stalks of wheat and sunflowers
And birds on invisible rods of glass
Flying over the top of the waters.
We two have become a group.

And we are not alone.
Our little group grows bigger.
By the dozens, dozens of dozens,
Hundreds of dozens,
They're hearing what we're doing.
Now they want to see,

A friendship fountain taking shape.
Getting ready for its voyage
From Atlantic shores to the Black Sea
And through the waters of Crimea.
Our symbol of solidarity with the
Freedom-loving people of Ukraine.

What to do when you are locked down by a heartless virus? PEG NICHOLS found it a perfect time to write a novel —*Sidewalk Sale Across America*—about how the Harkins try to hang on to family and livelihoods through a heartless virus. Peg Nichols is a long-time Kansas Authors Club member and member of the writing community in NE Kansas.

Peg Nichols believes the gift of a Friendship Fountain from the United States to Ukraine is a gesture the entire world would understand.

https://monarchbooksandgifts.com/

913-766-8646

MONARCH BOOKS & GIFTS

7713 W. 151st Street

Overland Park, KS

Symphony at Sundown:
Kelly W. Johnston

Alone at the ranch, I sit on the porch,
sip wine, and watch the sun sitting
on the horizon for a moment. Too long
I have been away in the city.

Not even a breeze rustles the grass.
The south pond is a mirror. I filled
the bird feeders first thing on arrival,
but they were long empty. The birds
are still unaware of new treasure.
I can hear the faint peeping of a small
bird in the tallgrass. A moment later,
a critter scratches in the dead leaves
beneath the hedgerow. A lone duck
hollers a hail call somewhere to the east.
Often, the sound of my pen moving across
paper is the only noise I notice.

I see a cottontail in the dimming light.
As quiet as rabbits are, I can still hear
dead grass crinkling with movement.
Bobcats know this is prime prowl time.
A flash of crimson sweeps before me -
three male cardinals appear by the feeder.
They chirp news of discovery of new seed.
I hear the three-note call of a barred owl,
then the yipping and howling of a pack
of coyotes is carried to me on south winds
and a pack to the west replies.
They keep yipping and locating –
a symphony at sundown.

KELLY W. JOHNSTON is a life-long Kansan who graduated from Wichita State University in 1977 while majoring in creative writing. He studied under A. G. Sobin, Anita Skeen and L. M. Grow. While at WSU, he published poems in *Mikrokosmos, The Cottonwood Review* and the *Ark River Review*. More recently, he has published poems in the *California Quarterly* (Vol. 43, #3), *The Flint Hills Review* and the *I-70 Review*. His chapbooks *Kalaska* (2017) and *Tumbleweed* (2021) were both published by the Blue Cedar Press. Kelly loves to spend time on his land in the Chautauqua Hills near Cross Timbers State Park where most of his poems have been inspired.

Solitude:
Ronda Miller

solitude
solidarity with nature
alone together

RONDA MILLER, Poetry Editor, is a Life Coach specializing in trauma. Miller teaches The Importance of Voice for Trauma Transformation in concert with The Johnson County Library, School of Trades and Department of Corrections. Her five books of poetry include: *Going Home: Poems from My Life*, *MoonStain*, *WaterSigns*, *Winds of Time* and *I Love the Child*.

RONDA MILLER, PHOTO

THE BUG DIARY

While experimenting with substances in the university library, Kymer is confronted by a ghost from KU's past: Carrie Watson, the librarian who is the library's namesake. Carrie gives Kymer the insect field journal of Flora Ellen Richardson, the first woman to graduate from KU. When Kymer reviews the bug diary, she realizes there's a bee in Flora's journal that's never before been identified by science. A wild ride ensues changing the world of entomology, and her personal world, forever.

The Bug Diary takes the reader on a wild review of history and bugs, and a laugh-out-loud exploration of campus life!

"Several supernatural episodes provide one catalyst for self-discovery... The characters feel real and lived-in, and some of the dialogue is downright hilarious. ... Fraley is a natural storyteller, and I am happy to follow wherever she leads." —*Karen M. Vaughn, author of* Death Comes for the Trophy Wife & Other Stories *and* A Kiss for a Dead Film Star and Other Stories

BARBARA WATERMAN PETERS, "SMILE"

A Murder at Radius:
Brenda White

Like crows we descend to
tables at Radius,
stretch our wings, touch beaks.

Our chatter is raucous.
We barely hear each other,
but we share tales of our flights,
bumpy or sublime,
the best trees and watering holes,
our favorite rooftops.

And on the luckiest nights,
we drop gifts on the table,
shiny pebbles, poems or prose,
bits and fancies scrawled on paper
like prisms or bells,
buttons, new pennies,
an odd-shaped stone.

We admire the plunder,
preen pieces and presenters,
caw our critiques, our counsel.
Then touching beaks and wingtips,
we all take flight,
disperse.

BRENDA L. WHITE is a native Emporian whose heart resides on acreage of the family farm in Morris county. An ex-opera student and cloth dollmaker, she is prone to talking to herself, to animals, and the occasional inanimate object. Her hobbies are daydreaming and watching snails. Brenda is a graduate of ESU. Her work has appeared in *Quivera*, *The Flint Hills Review*, *The Write Bridge*, and *Meadowlark 105 Reader*.

A Moment Behind
Two Eyes Draining:
Thaddeus Dugan

Tell me how
to carry, the burden
of this breath
when the air is heavy
& I don't know what to do.

When our hold on this world
comes into question,
as death rushes in
& waves distort my view.

This year has been surreal
with everyone around me
dropping like confetti.

As leaves fall
when their lease is up
the deceased crumble too.

Into the wind
the rigor of my mettle
grows dim,
as fumes fill
the seclusion of a room.

& then,
as if on cue
the seasoned spirit
ascends.

I shine in dim places
don't you forget

where you come from
what you have overcome
& if you loose it.
Everyone else will fall down too.

The poetry collection, *A Record Of Change*, was an Amity Literary Prize finalist in 2023. THADDEUS DUGAN resides in Topeka, Kansas and studies English/Writing at Washburn University. He has two cats, one named Araya and the other Eliot, who supervise all his writing endeavors. In his spare time he likes to read, write and observe all the conditions of the human experience. Find him on Facebook as TA Dugan or Thaddeus A Dugan, Author.

A RECORD OF CHANGE

Dugan's debut collection explores the evolution of the soul when age can no longer be used as an excuse not to change or when the pain becomes too great to remain the same. These poems reflect the rigorous self-examination it takes to reinvent yourself. Through love, grief, and loss The author does this, while never losing sight of his collective humanness.

"Attuned to the bluesy frequency of both inner and outer life, Dugan gives us a prescription. In this case, it is his poems—full of grit and softness, darkness and light. Give it a listen. It will help."
—*Kevin Rabas, Poet Laureate of Kansas (2017-2019), Improvise*

Thaddeus A. Dugan

Partitions - *Divided*:
Stephanie A. Barrows

Kurdish villages
On the border, divided
By outside forces –

Families, lives torn
By others' fears, hatred, lust;
An ancient story:

Iraq and Turkey
India and Pakistan
Ireland, Great Britain

Old South Africa
"Indian" reservations
"Race" segregation –

Human tragedies
Created by others' fears
Of a peaceful union.

Stephanie A. Barrows is an imaginative poet, musician, and artist. Her work aims to foster healing and inspire audiences to think in new ways about our relationships with our planet, ourselves and each other. You can find her improvising on flute and dancing to her heart's content in Lawrence, Kansas.

None of Us:
Diane Silver

Every kid who suspects they're the lost
prince or princess, every child who thinks
she must be an alien baby left by mistake,
knows the truth.

Even rich, white men with Brad Pitt faces,
overfilled trophy cases must know what
we're all afraid to say: None of us belongs

in this house at this time with these folks,
in this job in these clothes we've carefully
constructed to be a mirage.

A coworker said she must have missed
school the day they taught how to make
friends. Everyone nodded. I didn't.

I pursued the party pack, half a step back.
When the giddy kids paused, I slipped in,
lowered my voice, tamped down thoughts,
laughed even though my stomach hurt.

My gut sent me a message I couldn't read.
Even if I'd understood, I wouldn't have
believed. Square pegs desperate to fit in
round holes make themselves bleed.

DIANE SILVER is a Pushcart Prize-nominated poet who seeks to tease open the scars that life layers over our hearts. She retired recently after working in journalism, politics, and higher education. She publishes an essay every week about poetry and life at DianeSilver.substack.com.

Flirt - Identity:
Ronda Miller

Age ten, ribboned cigarette smoke entwined whispers
drift past easy bantering between bible camp kitchen-crew
teens. Casual toying, unwittingly inhaled, woven
into the preteen's forever yearn. Adult longings,
tucked inside self doubt, stir. Wanderlust, an
awkward girl/boy, child precariously perched,
isolated, teetering back and forth, wanting
first one identity, then the other. Not knowing
how to achieve either. Alienated, long legs
belying childhood curling discreetly beneath
a knee length yellow dress, bible open,
nervous fingers fiddling page corners.
"Big boys don't cry. Big boys don't cry.
I'm not in love. I'm not in love, just because,"
playing on the radio.

Here For You:
Heather Duris

I'll stand, just here.
A space away from you my friend
To let you breathe.
I'll give you space until you want less.
Or more of me.
I can't feel what you feel or know your thoughts,
but I'll share your space as near or far as you need.
If I could tie up broken pieces, soothe the raw spaces,
I would.
If I could put a bird's song inside your heart
I would.
I can only offer my feeble presence.
And a comforting embrace if you want it.
I'm here.

HEATHER DURIS is an artist living in Lawrence, Kansas. She studied art at the University of Missouri-Kansas City and then enlisted in the US Army as a Multimedia Illustrator. After three years in the Army Reserves and four years on active duty, Heather moved to Lawrence and attended the University of Kansas where she studied painting and art history. Heather makes jewelry, paints and has recently started making linocut prints. She is inspired by wild nature and the open landscapes of the prairie. Her style ranges from abstract landscapes to completely abstract expressions in color and shape. Her favorite artists include Henri Matisse, Helen Frankenthaler, Jean-Michel Basquiat and Raoul Dufy. heatherdurisart@gmail.com, facebook.com/HeatherDurisArt, Instagram.com/HeatherDurisArt, Heatherduris.substack.com

Helpers Hiding in Plain Sight:
Beth Gulley

Look for the helpers,
Mr. Rogers said,
when you need hope
in a horrible situation.

This morning amid
news of the war
between Hamas
and Israel
and the perennial
crush of the end
of fall semester,
helpers peek from
behind the scenes.

Jordanian soldiers,
famous for carrying
Syrian grandmothers
through no man's land
to safety from ISIS,
once again appear
on the scene
with a field hospital
to set up in Gaza
while by all appearances
no one else is doing anything
to help civilian Palestinians.

And in Introduction
to Writing class
a desperate student
who has failed
at both getting his keys

out of the car
before he locked it
and bringing money
to buy gas,
makes it to class just
in time to tell his story
before it's time to leave.

But a student
from across the room
hands over his last five dollars
to keep a fellow human
from being stuck.

Helpers hang out
in the margins
hiding in plain sight.

BETH GULLEY was an Amity literary prize finalist in 2023. The contest is sponsored by Anamcara Press. Beth Gulley lives in Spring Hill, Kansas and teaches writing at Johnson County Community College. She has published two chapbooks and three full-length collections of poetry: *Since Corona Ruined Our Trip to the Library* (Finishing Line Press), *Little Fish: Tiny Meditations on Freedom* (Flying Ketchup Press), *Dragon Eggs* (Spartan Press), *The Sticky Note Alphabet* (Alien Buddha Press), and *Love of Ornamental Fish* (Alien Buddha). Beth serves on the Riverfront Reading Committee and is a Writer's Place board member where she edits the yearbook. More information about Beth can be found on her blog at https://timeeasesallthings.wordpress.com/.

Dress For Succession:
Julie Ann Baker Brin

So, basically, everyone I know wants to be
cremated. Thank goodness, because I couldn't
handle the irresponsibility of discarding
a fine item of apparel that could otherwise be given
a new life, another purpose, a second chance.

Fabrics can last longer than our own tissues
if we take good care of them—isn't that odd?
Why wait for the anthropologists, the archaeologists,
the historians to tell those tales? Why occupy
so much finite space that could be used

by the ever multiplying living? I mean
no disrespect for any body. When I depart
this plane, I know I truly cannot take anything
with me. Let my shell grow moss, flowers, trees; let it be
given new life, another purpose, a second chance.

By day, JULIE ANN BAKER BRIN works in broadcasting: not behind a mic, but behind red tape. By night, she prefers to use the other brain hemisphere. She's an award-winning Kansas Authors Club member. JulieBrin.org showcases her works from *105 Meadowlark Reader*, Flying Ketchup's *Night Forest*, WSU's *Mikrokosmos* and more.

The Glacier Rock:
Shelley Watts Barnhill

Push, Push,
Scrape, scrape, along the earth.
Ice turns to water, trickles down, down seeking and finding the smallest crack in the hard granite.
Settles in and waits for bitter cold.
Freezes and expands.
Waits for more water to join, while above the pressure increases.
Freezes and expands… Freezes and expands.
Time moves on and so inevitably does the granite, a glacier remnant.
Rolling, scraping down the land heading south far away from where it broke from the earth.
Stops in soft soil, where an ancient seabed slumbers in the dryness of a prairie.

A man sees the usefulness of the traveler, the stone that has journeyed a thousand miles.
He hefts up and takes to a new resting place,
There the ruddy rock waits in both solitude and solidarity in the wall. Surrounded by limey friends.

One day I saw the well-travelled bit of granite which survived a difficult journey.
And thought "That rock is a lot like me, a visitor who stopped,
nestled in and found strength and purpose.
Here and now, it is my home."

This stone is in a wall on the southwest corner of Lawrence Avenue and West Sixth Street in Lawrence, Kansas. When I pass it as I have for over thirty years I reflect on its journey and how it is a bit like me.

GAROLD SNEEGAS, PHOTO

PART III:
TALL TALES,
SHORT STORIES
& ONE ACT PLAYS

YARNS

Fiction submitted for the Winter 2023/2024 edition of *The Write Bridge* include a stop at the Blue Moon cafe, a fear of the sky, counting on second chances, and the opportunity afforded by a storm. Surprise awaits the reader in *Orestes and the Flowerpunks*, by Connlyn Synclair, and *The Garden of Eden/Eatin*, by former Kansas Poet Laureate Kevin Rabas.

Watermark Bookstore

Since 1977, Watermark Books & Café has been Wichita's Home for Books. As a local business, we value our customers whether online or in the store. Beyond selling books and welcoming you in the café to meet (or make) a friend over coffee or lunch, we connect to the community through donations, in-kind, volunteer, or financial. We sponsor author events featuring bestselling and soon-to-be-bestselling authors. We collaborate with non-profits, other local businesses, schools, churches, libraries, and other organizations that make our community what it is. Since 1996, we have been an anchor for the Lincoln Heights Village Shopping Center at the southwest corner of Douglas and Oliver.

Kim:
Brian Daldorph

We stop off in the Blue Moon Café for coffee and donuts at 11.11 p.m. It's a warm summer night and we're so happy together we don't want the night to end. Kim points to one donut then another behind the glass: "That one! No, that one! I can't make up my mind!" She asks for water, not coffee: "Or else I won't be able to sleep tonight!"

We've just been to see *Chariots of Fire,* about British runners in the Olympics before the war, the film everyone's talking about though I could hardly watch it because—for the first time—Kim and I held hands and I'm not even sure how it happened, did my hand creep into her hand or was it the other way around?

We're first-year college students and met at Community Action Club. We both want to do things to help make the world a better place.

Kim and I sit with our donuts and drinks and she starts telling me that her parents and sister will be coming to visit her: "I want you to meet them!"

What I don't know at this point in a late-night café in college town is that pretty soon after I will make a mess of my life when I fall under the sway of Julia, who will always have packets of pills in her pockets and a stash of dope in her room and will invite me into her bed on our first night together.

Julia will get me hooked and we'll go crazy, wreck her car, end up in hospital with a lot of pain meds in our blood.

I'll drop out of school, go home, take a shit job, find a dealer, live my life trying to get high, do some jail time then prison.

I'll lose touch with Kim, of course, though I'll find out by chance years later that she married a lawyer and started her own ad agency.

But there was that one night together in the Blue Moon when we ate donuts and everything was sweet, so very sweet.

BRIAN DALDORPH teaches at the University of Kansas and Douglas County Jail. He edits Coal City Review. His most recent books of poetry are Ice Age/ Edad de Hielo (Irrupciones P, 2017), Blue Notes (Dionysia P, 2019), and Kansas Poems (Meadowlark P, 2021).

Sky Child:
Lori Stratton

She was born in a place where the sky stretched from one edge of the brown and green land to the other. People just passing through couldn't understand such a sky, and they grew frightened by it.

"It's like being on an island," they'd say, although most of them had never experienced that, either. "Too much sky. You could drown in it."

But Elsie grew up addicted to the sky, much like those born on an island grew up addicted to the smell of sea spray, the feel of sand under their toes. Hers was a childhood full of wind, and sun, and clouds that floated across the sky like puffs of cotton candy. She spent her days meandering through the fields, singing with the meadowlarks, hugging the breeze.

Because she was their first, then sadly, their only child, her parents knew no differently, yet they feared. They would watch their daughter, her straight, silvery hair flying out from her face, her eyes almost translucent in their blueness, and they knew she could see what they couldn't. Elsie would spread her thin arms wide, embrace the sky and twirl, first slowly, then faster, spinning in circles for hours.

"She will be an artist," they said to each other, with a bravado that never penetrated the shakiness in their voices.

They hoped their daughter's love of sky would transmute into creativity, and they waited for her to begin painting, to start writing. They tried dance lessons, then the violin. But none of the lessons lasted long, and the teachers would bring Elsie out to her waiting parents who always sat immobile, sun-speckled hands folded on their laps.

"Not for her," the teachers would say, shaking their heads, and the parents saw the pity hiding in the teachers' eyes.

So Elsie's parents grew fierce and protective and built an impenetrable shell around their daughter. But that was before they knew about the voices, of course.

The voices first spoke to Elsie when she turned five, the summer before she started school. They were lovely voices, full of tiny lights and tinkling bells. Elsie wanted no other playmates.

Full of mother-love and locked with Elsie inside a make-believe world, her mother would smile at her child, swallow her mother-fears, and pretend she was lucky to have such an easy daughter. Like her own calloused feet, Elsie's mother was heavy, thick with farm work and struggle, and she rejoiced in Elsie's lightness. So easy to please, always smiling.

But different thoughts nagged at Elsie's father, and he watched his silver child with unease, hoping she'd ask for a doll, a dog, an ice cream cone. He put up a swing set, doing what he always did, battling his fear by working with something heavy he could grasp with his hands.

Then Elsie went to school, and the horizon grew dark, ominous, full of storms. For hours each day she was a child shut off from the sky, and she'd sit at her desk, staring at the ceiling, willing the tiles and plaster and shingles to melt away. The voices she loved, which had always been kind before, became loud and brash, threatening and windy.

"Come back to us," they cried. "You must come back!"

Elsie couldn't ignore them. She'd stand by her desk or run to the door, screaming, with tears the color of her hair running down her cheeks.

And her teacher, new to this world of sky but not new to children, would take Elsie's hand and lead her back to her desk, drying her tears with a tissue.

"We need you here, Elsie," the teacher would say, and Elsie would look into her soft brown eyes and almost believe.

The days passed, and Elsie came to love her teacher almost as much as she loved the sky. When the teacher held her hand, leaned over her desk, and smiled into her eyes, the voices became quieter, almost silent. But when the teacher turned her back to help another child, the voices would scream out, and Elsie would run again.

The teacher called Elsie's parents, and they felt no surprise when she told them they needed to speak. Their hope disappeared as they walked with leaden feet into the school's corridor, each clutching one of Elsie's hands. Once in the room, Elsie went to the window and began drawing circles with her right index finger, her skin skimming the glass.

"Elsie has pretend friends," the teacher said, looking straight into the eyes of Elsie's father. "But she believes they are real. She hears their voices. Sometimes she talks to them during class, as if they are sitting right beside her, or rather, hovering directly over her. It's very distracting to the other students."

The teacher paused, noticing their pain, and feeling the sudden guilt of being glad Elsie wasn't her child. They had not warned her of this in the teachers' college.

"I'm sorry."

Elsie's mother smiled and nodded, denying what had to be true, what she had seen for herself. And Elsie's father, who tilled the earth for a living, knew what had to be done. He shook the teacher's soft hand and put on his worn baseball cap.

They took Elsie to the city, three hours away by car, to a place filled with concrete and glass buildings. Elsie strained to see over the buildings, and she stumbled as she looked up. She was suffocating, and she pulled on her mother's arm.

"I can't breathe," Elsie said, gasping. "Please, let's leave."

Veiled behind a thick layer of sadness, Elsie's mother patted her shoulder. "We're almost there, sweetheart. We're almost there."

They entered a red brick building and Elsie felt relief, for a moment, from the grayness. They waited in a carpeted room with three-month-old issues of *People Magazine* and *The Saturday Evening Post*. Finally, a stout nurse ushered them in to see the doctors, an owl-faced man whom Elsie instinctively disliked, and then another, a woman, brown all over. There were tests, and games, and questions, and Elsie listened for the voices.

"Unsafe here," the voices chimed. "Get out, get out."

Finally the owl-faced doctor pulled her parents into his tired office.

"Schizophrenia," he said. "Unusual for one so young, but not unheard of. The signs are all there."

His eyes blinked behind his round spectacles. He thought of the weekend, of his wife's apple strudel, of anything except the heavy faces of those who sat before him.

The brown doctor nodded in agreement, and sent Elsie home with two white bottles, one full of pink pills, and the other, purple ones.

At first, Elsie refused to take the pills, despite the fact that her mother pleaded with her, offering all sorts of treats: ice cream, chocolate, a trip to the movies, a kitten. But Elsie had never been one to care much about the world's enticements, and she shut her mouth and leaned toward the voices.

Her father's eyes grew hard and his mouth straight, and he refused to bargain. He held Elsie's arms with one large hand, pried her mouth open with the other.

"Give them to her," he commanded his wife, who poked first a pink pill and then a purple one inside.

"Swallow," he said, and Elsie did, despite herself.

From then on, Elsie took the pills, because her earth-father wouldn't let her outside if she didn't. He nailed her window shut, glued the blind to the window sill. He had become her jailer, her captor and enemy, all softness in him disappeared. She swallowed the poison that silenced her friends, but still she could reach them, could feel their presence as the breeze brushed across her cheek.

"Come back to us," she thought she heard them say. "Come back."

School became easier, and teachers stayed kind. There were even some friends, a shy girl named Chrissy, and Derrick, a boy with bright red hair. Despite the pills, the teachers, the sometimes-friends, Elsie knew she belonged to a different place. She'd retreat to her world at night in her bedroom, tired of pretending on this earth, and she'd twirl in circles, her nightgown swirling out from her bare legs. She'd imagine the sun warming her face, and peace would finally descend.

* * * * *

Many years later, after graduation, Elsie didn't leave that place of sky as almost everyone else did. Chrissy first, then Derrick, and then the phone stopped ringing altogether. During the evenings, her father would pore over brochures from cosmetology schools and community colleges, trying to find a place for Elsie to belong. Elsie smiled to herself, because she knew exactly where she belonged.

She would float from one room to another, humming and pretending her parents didn't exist. Her mother smiled, too, happy that her sky-child still needed her. But her father would set down the brochures and watch Elsie, anger in his eyes and sorrow in his heart.

When Frank came, Elsie didn't notice him at first, because she thought he belonged to the earth, like her father. Frank sold implements, tools, metal that sliced into dirt. But she soon found out that he was trapped on the ground like her.

He began to speak to her, to arrive just as supper was being set on the table, to take her outside in the evenings and admire her as she twirled in the yard. Elsie could see in the blueness of Frank's eyes, feel in the softness of his lips upon hers, that he, also, was made of sky, and happiness overcame her.

Her father and mother breathed a collective, satisfied sigh, she because Elsie and Frank went to the courthouse and then to a small house only a few miles away, and Elsie's father because his silver sky-child had finally become someone else's burden.

It was bliss at first, and Frank would laugh as he came home to dinners of marshmallows and ice cream, vanilla pudding and whipped topping.

By the time the baby came, however, Frank had grown tired. Elsie had to quit taking the pink and purple poison, it wasn't good for the baby, the doctor said, and pretending wasn't fun anymore. Then the final day arrived when he came home to find Elsie dancing naked in the field while the baby, a round pink bundle, screamed in the bassinet.

"That's it," Frank had said, picking up the diaper bag, the screaming infant, and his wife, and depositing them into his four-door sedan.

"I can't do it anymore," he told his father-in-law, standing on the dusty porch of Elsie's parents' farmhouse, his toe drawing an invisible line. "I've tried. Really, I have."

Elsie's father nodded, feeling heavy with the knowledge, but understanding. Frank got into the sedan and drove off without looking back.

So Elsie's parents began tending to two sky-daughters, which ended up being not much more difficult than taking care of just one. And Elsie began the pills again, first the pink, then the purple, and the baby grew round and happy.

It was in the spring of that year when Elsie's mother returned from hanging a load of laundry on the clothesline to find Elsie in the bathtub, looking out the window and trailing her fingers in the water while the pink baby quietly drowned. It was too late to save the infant, and Elsie's mother at last felt the true pain of giving birth to a sky-daughter.

When the sheriff came, he found the pills, too many to count, in a clear glass jar inside the drawer in Elsie's nightstand. She had learned not to swallow them, to put them in her mouth and then to spit them out later.

"They sparkle," she said, taking the jar from the sheriff's roughened hand, "when you hold them up to the sun. See?"

Now Elsie lives in a place where there is no sky. She spends her day walking from one gray room to another, although sometimes the walls are white. The pills have transformed into shots, given each day by strange men and women with feet made of clay. But when she strains, when she really, really tries, Elsie can still hear the voices.

And then she smiles because she knows what the others, those made of earth, will never learn. The sky really exists inside of her. The others think she lives in a gray room, but she doesn't.

The sky has combined with her soul, and Elsie twirls forever, her silver hair streaming behind her like wispy clouds.

LORI STRATTON is a high school English teacher who writes creative non-fiction, short stories, and the occasional poem. She also works at the intersection of education policy and racial and social justice through the National Education Association's Leaders for Just Schools. She has a journalism degree through the University of Kansas, and has been a National Board Certified teacher since 2006. She lives in Lawrence, Kansas, with her husband, where they enjoy frequent visits from their three young adult children and their four grandchildren.

The Fall of Bellwether

Broughman has created an American epic, a grand story that stretches across land and water, time and race, gender and religion. ... as characters go off to war, flee to cities, and escape the terrors of slavery, we encounter the awesome forces of mercy, hope, even forgiveness. Broughman's prose sweeps from achingly tender to brutal and bare-knuckled, his prowess managing multiple voices and tensions. ...brazenly beautiful writing. —*John Mauk, author of Field Notes for the Earthbound*

Chad V. Broughman

"Chad Broughman's debut novel is as beautiful as it is brutal, a tale of small-minded evil and redemption set in post-Civil War America. The Fall of Bellwether left me feeling like I'd just read a horror story wrapped in a lullaby. It's a page-turner that will stick with me forever." New York Times Bestselling Author Susan Donovan, *Take A Chance on Me*

Second Chances:
Bruce Rolfe

When Janey handed her pet bullfrog to Brett to keep for the weekend, he knew she was unlike any other girl. That had been back in preschool and was his earliest memory of the girl he played football and baseball with as a kid, dated throughout high school and college, and married the day after graduation. It only made good sense with both their families in town for the commencement ceremony to have them stay over and share the union of their lives.

"I'm pregnant," she said, five months later as they cuddled together in front of an artificial fireplace in their small one-bedroom apartment. "How does it feel to know you're going to be a father?"

Being in love with Janey just kept getting better and better. "I couldn't be happier," he said before dashing off to Dairy Queen for a package of Dilly Bars to celebrate with. When he returned home with the ice cream treat their front door was standing open and his pretty wife was dead.

That was twelve years ago and not a day went by that Brett didn't think of Janey and how their life might have been if she hadn't been taken from him so suddenly, so violently, and so senselessly. Although the police caught the man who did it and a jury convicted him and sentenced him to die by lethal injection, Janey's murderer lived all those years on death row filing appeal after appeal.

"How do you think I feel?" he said, shoving a cameraman out of his way as he exited the prison. Attending the execution hadn't brought the relief or closure he thought it might. His wife's murderer had just drifted off to sleep, his upper lip curled in a final remorseless sneer. It hardly seemed fair considering the pain and suffering he'd put them through.

Brett just couldn't answer anymore inane questions—choking on the words as if some jagged piece of glass was caught in his throat each time he tried to speak. He headed for the nearest bar—a crutch he hadn't allowed himself while remaining focused on making sure Janey's killer got what he deserved. He hadn't dated anyone during the past twelve years either, afraid to open himself up the way he had with Janey because it reminded him just how much he hurt inside.

"Well, hello there," said a bouncy redhead sitting at the bar as Brett walked in. She looked all cheesecaky like Marilyn Monroe singing "Happy Birthday" to President Kennedy he'd seen on the History Channel. She was also several years younger than he and obviously intoxicated—why else would a good-looking girl like her even notice him? In fact, he probably looked as bad as he felt after attending the execution and dodging reporters half the night.

"Hello there yourself," he said, sliding onto the barstool beside her and motioning to the bartender. He wasn't sure why he hadn't just walked to the other end and sat by himself, but the girl's cheerful smile seemed to be something he needed, and her scent was tantalizingly clean and fresh.

"I'm Noreen, Noreen Baker," she said, extending her hand, which had French manicured nails and a surprisingly strong grip . . . just like Janey's.

"Pleased to meet you, I'm—"

"—Brett Cunningham, I know."

He stared at her and ordered a shot of Old Granddad and a draught beer from the bartender who'd come over to take his order. Noreen was completely different from Janey who noticed other women and pointed them out to Brett. "Do you think she's pretty," she would say trying to elicit some response from him other than, "Not especially." Usually, top heavy women caught his wife's eye and Brett was sure that Janey would have noticed Noreen and pointed her out. But the truth was, when Janey was alive, he never would have given Noreen a second glance and he was sure that he'd passed many just as beautiful since then.

"I saw you on TV," Noreen said. "You really gave that reporter what he deserved."

He felt the heat rising past his collar. "I really lost it, didn't I?"

She patted his arm. "I probably would have done the same thing. It's understandable to want to leave painful memories undisturbed, but the questions journalists ask are seldom compatible with concern for the victim. In their eyes it's the man who was executed this evening who's the real story."

"That's ridiculous!"

"I'm sorry, but it's true. It's what they teach us."

"You a reporter?" Brett asked standing and backing away.

She grabbed his jacket. "I'm taking journalism in school. I've always wanted to be a reporter, but my husband thought I wasn't callous enough. 'It's way too dangerous,' he'd say. After watching you shove that reporter, I see what he meant."

Brett pulled away from her grasp and slapped a ten-dollar bill on the bar to pay for his drinks. "I told you; I lost it. Now, I think I'd better leave before I lose it again."

"I don't want a story, Mr. Cunningham; I want an education. I have a family to support and the fourth estate is where I've always wanted to work. I think that I can bring a little civility to the profession if you'll just give me half a chance. Please tell me about your wife. What was she like?"

"How did you know I'd be here?"

"I didn't. I don't even drink," she said, raising her glass. "Ginger Ale. For whatever reason, I was just sort of drawn here tonight."

"Yeah, like I'm supposed to believe that."

"It's true. I didn't follow you. I was here first, remember?"

Realizing that he hadn't had a drink in years himself he cautiously reseated himself beside her. "So, why do you want to know about Janey?"

"I don't know, I just do."

"Off the record?"

"Strictly."

He reached for his beer, but she stopped him. "I want to

hear from you, not the booze."

He nodded and began talking about Janey, slowly at first, then gushing over the smallest details until he got to the part about how his wife pointed out other women to him and that Noreen surely would have caught her eye. He was about to tell her how Janey would have queried him with, "Do you think she's pretty?" when he could have sworn he heard Janey say, "Go for it, Brett. I can't rest easy while your heart is still in pain."

"Last call," the bartender said as Brett glanced up into Noreen's turquoise eyes, feeling slightly embarrassed.

Noreen took out a felt-tip pen, wrote her telephone number on a bar napkin, and slid it in front of him. "I've had a wonderful evening, Brett. Call me. I'd love to talk with you some more. Janey sounds like a wonderful person—a true soul mate if there ever was one. I know I would have liked her a lot. But next time, I want to hear about you."

A spark jumped from her fingertips and nipped the back of his hand as she slid off the barstool.

She smiled and a lump formed in his throat. Where had the evening gone? He didn't remember her saying a word but obviously she had because he knew that Noreen was a single mother who'd lost her husband in a drunk-driving accident the night their little girl was born. He'd been out celebrating. How sad was that? And somewhere in the conversation Noreen had told him that although her husband hadn't had the reasons to drink that Brett might, she wouldn't consider seeing him again if he did. She couldn't put herself through something like that again—it was just too painful.

He glanced at the bar and realized that he hadn't touched his drinks. When he looked up again, Noreen was gone. Only her fragrance remained. Strangely, for the first time since Janey's murder all he could think about was Noreen and how alive she'd made him feel. Never before had he been able to discuss his innermost feelings with anyone besides Janey, yet for the past three hours he'd done precisely that with a total stranger. He glanced back at the napkin to make sure he wasn't dreaming. The number was written beneath a little bullfrog she'd sketched, and her scent was coming from the napkin. Smiling, he picked it up and tucked it in the shirt pocket over his heart.

BRUCE ROLFE, a former U.S. Navy Search & Rescue pilot for 20 years, is proud to say there are nine souls here today because he was there then. He is the author of the Chip Hale handyman series of mystery novels, *Tools of the Trade, Trademark of Murder*, and *Trade Secrets*. His next book, *Family Trade* is forthcoming. Bruce also has a new standalone book coming out from Dingbat Publishing. *The Little Storehouse in the Middle of the Block* is the memoir of a wannabe writer, who at 47, discovered after his mother's death that he was adopted, she was murdered, and his quest to find his biological parents. Find Bruce here: http://brucerolfe.com/

The Storm:
Gretchen Cassel Eick

It was raining with a vengeance and the lowered sky, coupled with the fact that she had never been here, made the old brick building appear threatening.

The Washington, D.C. office of Children's International occupied a three-story brownstone near Capitol Hill. The taxi driver's window wipers were working overtime as he pulled up to the rowhouse and squinted to make out the number. He mumbled something about the impossible sheets of rain pounding the sidewalk before he clicked the release on his trunk so she could retrieve her two bags. He didn't exit the car or help her lug her suitcases up the flight of stairs to the entrance. Before she reached the stoop, he was off, his tires throwing water that drenched the sidewalk, causing an umbrella'd woman walking past to swear at him.

She rang the bell and waited, then rang again, her coat peppered with dark spots. Water slid down her cheeks and dripped from her nose. She hoped they were open this early. She stood waiting for what seemed a long time. What would she do if no one was there?

"You'll catch your death of cold out here waterlogged and woebegone. Let me help you with that." An older woman had opened the door. She introduced herself as Sally Jones. She pulled one of the bags into the foyer and the woman followed her, dragging the other. Across the puddles forming around the bags, Sally's eyes curious.

"I'm Priscilla Musleh. I'm just returned from Gaza to bring you my report," the younger woman said, feeling as she said the words how incredible it was that she had made it out at all.

"Oh, yes! Welcome. You must be exhausted. And you're soaking wet! If you wait a moment, I'll fetch a towel ..." Sally brought two towels and Patricia dried her hair and face and her luggage before following Sally into a small waiting room.

"Can I get you a cup of coffee or tea?"

"Yes, please. That would be lovely. Coffee. With sugar, no cream. Thanks."

Sally returned with coffee and several cookies. "I told Mr. Kovich you're here. He'll come greet you as soon as he can. I'm afraid tonight is our big fund raiser, so things are rather hectic, and he is swamped with all the people calling to ask if the event has been canceled. We're worried the storm may cut into our attendance. Which would be a shame as we rely on tonight's fundraiser for revenue to do our work."

"Sally?" a voice called.

"I'm sorry but I need to go." Sally hurried down the hallway.

Sinking into a chair, Priscilla opened her roller bag and retrieved a dry pair of socks and shoes. Closing her eyes, she listened to the sounds of the building—footsteps on the bare wood floors, clicking computer keys, voices on telephones, and, muting everything, the rain.

She was exhausted. And depressed. As low as she had ever felt in her entire life, if she was honest with herself.

She had fallen asleep when, twenty minutes later, Mr. Kovich entered the room. He was about her age, fifty-ish, and his face looked care-worn, like someone who tried to carry the weight of the world's suffering. She noticed that he had a habit of running his fingers through his hair. It rose up from his scalp like a rock star's, but she doubted this man used hair gel. It gave him a surprised look that amused her.

"Ms. Musleh? I'm terribly sorry to have kept you waiting. I had forgotten you were coming today." He approached and assessed whether to take her hand, given her Muslim surname. When she extended her own, he took it in both of his. "We're rather overwhelmed with preparations for tonight." He seated himself on the sofa and peered earnestly at her. "How was your trip?"

She didn't speak of the flight from Cairo to D.C. but of what she had seen in Gaza. It poured out of her. The orphanage beside her mother-in-law's home that ran out of blankets and food. The children's hospital in Gaza City that the Israelis had bombed. The people like her husband's uncle who were hospitalized when the assault began and could not be moved, despite the Israeli government insisting everyone must leave the north and move into the south.

She rummaged in her bag and brought out the folio of photos she'd taken, passing them to him one at a time as she narrated what they depicted. He sat beside her looking at each image, intent and frowning. He seemed genuinely distressed by the photos of children half buried in rubble or wrapped in shrouds for burial, old people weeping as they huddled beside the one remaining wall of their home, mass graves on the compound of Shifa Hospital, young men, themselves survivors, digging for signs of life. He asked her questions and listened carefully. She felt a surge of gratitude for his attentiveness and concern. After eight weeks of drone attacks and bombing, she had begun to despair if anyone cared.

Thunder, and then loud cracks of lightning, interrupted their conversation, causing her to crouch, hands over her head. He placed his hand on her shoulder as though he understood her response.

He returned to studying her report, shaking his head as he let himself feel what he was reading and seeing. He took time he had said he didn't have today. When he looked up at her, his eyes were soft. "Working in a war zone is terribly difficult." He spoke deliberately. "You've done well. And I'm sure it has taken its toll on you. Thank you for making the effort to bring this to us so quickly." He shifted position, paused, and changed the subject. "Are you staying in D.C. long?"

"I have a plane to catch to Chicago this afternoon at 4:30… My mother's expecting me. She's been worried," she replied.

"Understandably. But if the storm is as bad as they're predicting, your flight may be canceled. If that happens, I hope you will stay here. We have a room with a bath upstairs. Plenty of blankets and food." He seemed to be a kind person.

When Beethoven's 5th sounded from his phone, he stood. "I'm sorry I can't stay to talk with you longer. I must attend to more details for tonight. Are you comfortable waiting here until you leave for Reagan Airport?" At her nod, he walked to the door, turned, and threw her a smile of encouragement before hurrying down the stairs.

When Sally returned, she asked how Priscilla had become an aid worker for Children's International. She, too, and listened carefully.

"My husband was from Palestine—from Gaza, not the West Bank. We met in Chicago while we were both in grad school studying journalism and we married and stayed in the U.S. He went back to visit his family in 2016. You may remember that Israel invaded Gaza that year. Which happened just after he arrived in Gaza City... He was killed. We think he was targeted as a journalist."

Priscilla turned her face away for a few moments and took a deep breath. "I knew I had to find meaningful employment or my grief would have buried me, so I contacted a number of organizations working in the region. I was afraid to be a journalist, working with children sounded safer. And a few weeks after I sent you my application, you hired me!"

"Do you have children?"

"No. We tried for years. I had four miscarriages. Maybe that's why I wanted to work for children." She forced a smile.

"How did you happen to be in Gaza this fall?"

"Three months ago, I was visiting my husband's family in the north of Gaza and investigating conditions in Gaza for children. I was there when Hamas raided Israel on October 7th and killed 1,200 Israelis. Immediately the Israelis attacked Gaza with drones and bombing. They said we must leave the north or be bombed. But we couldn't leave. They bombed the highway to the south. Gaza is only twenty-five miles long and six miles wide, but it is enclosed in a wall. With no border crossing open, there was nowhere to go. People were stuck."

Priscilla paused. "The carnage was like nothing I have ever seen. Even as a U.S. citizen I couldn't get out, not for two months. I'm very lucky I wasn't killed along with the 14,000 that were dead by the time I left."

In her mind Priscilla saw the streets filled with refugees and her husband's father pushing his brother who they had taken from the hospital through the rubble in a wheelchair. People walking. No cars. There was no gasoline. Here and there a donkey harnessed to a makeshift cart that held a family and all they could carry.

"My husband's family had to flee their home to escape the bombing and find food and water...."

She was talking so fast she was out of breath. There had been no one to talk with about what was happening in Palestine after she left. And she urgently needed to talk. Early in their marriage she and Ali had covered another war zone, and she'd learned that she must abbreviate her words, or the listener could not take it in. Perhaps she had already exceeded Sally's capacity to absorb this? She tried to conclude her story.

"I got out four days ago through the Rafah crossing into Egypt, the only way one can get out. I caught a flight from Cairo to Washington to bring you my report and my photos. I guess I could have express mailed them, but I needed to come myself."

Sally studied Priscilla's devastated face in silence before touching her arm in sympathy. "Mr. Kovich has a similar story. This work has been his salvation, like it was yours."

Hail pounding the window drew their eyes to the storm raging outside this cozy room. Sally appeared suddenly distracted.

"That sounds worrisome. Who will come tonight if it is storming like this? Anyway, let me take you to our room upstairs where you can rest and be more comfortable." Sally picked up Priscilla's roller bag and led the way upstairs to a back room with a cot, an overstuffed chair, a reading lamp, and a lavatory. "Mr. Kovich stays here often," she said. "Workaholic."

Priscilla's phone binged announcing a text from United Airlines. She sank onto the cot. "My flight was canceled!"

"I am so sorry. You're probably eager to get home. I'll get some blankets. And a sandwich. You can call home and tell your mom. It will be all right."

Alone, Priscilla opened her bags and took out her

belongings, savoring the memories they brought of Ali's family, pushing away the other, horrific memories that crowded her brain.

She looked up to see Mr. Kovich in the doorway watching her. He looked glad to see her there. "I just heard your flight was canceled. Please do stay with us. You can attend our fundraiser—and enjoy a fine catered meal… And you can pad our attendance numbers!" He grinned conspiratorially.

He paused and then stepped into the room, studying her closely. "Sally told me your story. I'm very sorry. One wonders if one's grief will ever end."

His kindness and the sadness on his face made her want very much for it to end for him. And for her. She replied: "People tell me there comes a time when we are surprised by joy again. But we must wait for it. We can't push the river."

"C. S. Lewis and Frederick Buechner! Their books have brought me through many long nights. You, too?"

She nodded.

"You wonder why you are still here in the face of so much loss. You don't know what to do and grief numbs you." He looked at her to see if she understood.

Eyes wet she mumbled, "Yes."

In that moment something changed.

As they acknowledged the pain of their solitude and isolation, the pain of overwhelming losses, something new seemed to open before them. Not a cavern or a pit, but the fragile possibility of new life. Simultaneously they smiled.

Sally brought sandwiches and they munched and talked of happier times in their lives. It felt comfortable, even "easy," although both were more familiar with "hard." Sometime later they noticed that the storm had quieted.

Sally knocked on the door jamb. "NPR just announced that planes are flying again from Reagan. Check your airline. Maybe you can get to Chicago after all."

Priscilla pulled out her phone and entered her code.

Mr. Kovich knelt to help refill her suitcases. His eyes avoided hers. Still holding her open phone she knelt and joined him in repacking. She could feel the warmth of his body beside hers.

He smelled pleasantly of Ivory soap and aftershave.

She closed her phone.

He looked at her, questioning.

"Maybe I should stay," she said.

She left the suitcase half-packed and took a deep breath. Her voice sounded unsteady and tentative. "One thing I learned in the past eight weeks: life is short, and you can't count on tomorrow. I'll never find joy again if I can't take the risk of more loss."

Mr. Kovich's smile lit the room. "Perhaps this could be that time."

Visiting and living in other countries shapes Gretchen's life. She taught in Latvia and Bosnia and Herzegovina and worked for 14 years as a foreign policy lobbyist. She wrote two award-winning scholarly histories and five novels (the latest, *Dark Crossings,* 2022). She was Kansas Authors Club's Prose Writer of 2021.

Twice Told Tales

104 South Main Street

McPherson, KS 67460

(620) 718-5023

Orestes and The Flowerpunks:
Connlyn Synclair

Reporter Johnny Orestes was always sent to cover any controversy which involved colleges, including college sports. His editor thought that by virtue of a surname acquired by a grandfather with a devotion for classicalism that he'd be able to get wizened old professors to reveal things they otherwise wouldn't to a reporter.

Today he was standing comfortably in the east library of Northwestern Kansas College of Arts and Agriculture waiting to talk to a professor of literature who doubled as a spokesman.

Outside several dozen flowerpunks, the newest and most numerous punk subculture, were occupying the main campus. They carried protest signs and waved flags adorned with abstract flowers and insects. Classes hadn't been canceled, of course, but no one showed up.

Like most colleges in suburbia, Northwestern Ag, as it was called, was made up of a section of residential neighborhoods donated by the developer to the cause of higher education for the much loved tax breaks it granted them. In this case, three consecutive blocks complete with three cul-de-sacs where the asphalt had been torn up and replaced with experimental gardens.

The occupying force seemed to shy away from the gardens and were concentrated on singing protest songs in the street, marching from one end of campus to the other.

"Mister Orestes was it? From *The Weekly Athenian?* I'm Professor Argo, would you like a glass of juice?" Argo was a little man of about 50 with large black-framed glasses.

"No. Thank you though." Orestes said politely.

"I don't know what more I can tell you. As I told the *Colby Tribune*, Doctor Menelaus Stross has an exemplary record with the Colorado National Guard and is considered by many an expert in gene based pesticide development. These hooligans call him a fascist but they're the ones who have forced us to shut the campus down?"

"I want to make sure I understand, you have no plans to ask for police involvement?" Johnny asked.

"No. No! And I want to make it clear we will not call in a neighborhood watch either! It's our belief that these 'flower people' will come to their senses as long as we don't engage with them. Now please excuse me." Argo said and left.

Johnny had hoped Argo had a statement to give to the protestors, but it seemed the college was feeling the heat. To the old school of academia, with their devotion to classicalism and the often right-wing paramilitary, neighborhood watches were a symbol of the ills of modern society, but Stross had connections to several and only that could have prompted a fussy little man like Argo to even bring the subject up.

Johnny slipped on a pair of shades and exited the library into the hot September air. Since he'd otherwise struck out with Argo, he'd try to get a few quotes from the protestors and then go home.

It would be social suicide for a nice classically educated young man like himself to say it out loud, but he admired the flowerpunks. He might have thought their costumes were silly, but they had more guts than most suburbanites. As a journalist, though, he had to maintain the appearance of having no biases at all.

Johnny decided to take a detour to catch a glimpse of one of the exotic experimental gardens but when he got to the garden's edge he saw something incredible.

On the ground was a flowerpunk clad in a bright red beret and matching trench coat stained with the darker red of blood, and standing above him was Doctor Menelaus Stross, holding a metallic army issue pistol.

"Who the hell are you!?" Stross shouted. He raised the gun to point it at Johnny, but noticed his press badge and dropped the gun.

"It was self defense! I was thinking about my plans for the garden when he came at me with that club!" Stross added quickly.

Johnny bent down again to look at the body; there was indeed a walking stick covered in carvings of flowers. It was both good hardwood and well carved. If it wasn't homemade, it would have cost a fortune.

"I'll go get Professor Argo so he can call the police. It's not my place, and probably best for you if you don't do it either," Johnny replied, looking back up at the nervous, fidgety Professor Stross.

Within thirty minutes four state troopers showed up and began taping off the area around the garden. Johnny knew they'd want to interview him, so he decided to stand off to the side and review what he knew about Stross. The internet was one of the things about the old, urbanized world which pretty much everyone was glad was still around.

According to the blog posts Johnny had bookmarked, Stross had been a national guard medic with connections to several neighborhood watches around the Kansas/Colorado border but had left the service two years short of retirement to work for a company that researched gene-based pesticides. Strange qualifications for a teacher, but it got more bizarre according to some. People said that his company was a front for the CIA, and Stross's real work was with biological weapons.

Johnny thought it was nonsense. The story had clearly been bought by the impressionable teenagers who made up the flowerpunks, but in all honesty, even if the CIA still existed, it had to pay better than Northwestern Ag. Besides, even pushing fifty, a guy with army and CIA training wouldn't be too threatened by a twenty-something with a big stick.

A twenty-something with a stick Stross conveniently had a pistol to blow away at point blank range. *Why wait until he was right in front of him?* Johnny frowned. He was beginning think there was something more going on.

Johnny, as a matter of procedure, called the office of the

chancellor and left a message asking for any comment on the shooting and whether it had any effect on Stross's employment with the college. He wasn't expecting a reply. The chancellor, like Argo, was a classically educated academic, and Johnny knew that they hated nothing more than controversy which was 'common' or 'crass.'

His best bet was to get the story of the other side, but he wasn't under any delusion that the flowerpunks were going to be any easier to get on record.

The flowerpunks had found out about the shooting from the state troopers. The troopers were not feeling sympathetic because they hadn't been called in to disperse the crowd earlier. The college refused to press charges, so the protesters still occupied the main street singing protest songs about non-conformists who met sticky ends. The armed police were standing by in case things turned violent. There was no trust lost between both groups.

Johnny showed his press badge to the police and walked up to a group of singing flowerpunks; the singing stopped and they looked at him. Clearly they thought of him as an enemy who represented suburbia.

"I'm Johnny Orestes, reporter for the *Weekly Athenian.* One of your comrades was shot…"

"Murdered by that fascist pig, Stross!" someone interjected.

"He very well might have been. Questions need to be asked. Questions that the police aren't going to be in a rush to ask themselves. If some of you will go on the record about what's happened…" Johnny continued raising his voice to try and address the entire crowd.

"No way! You've got a classical name. You don't have any sympathy for us!"

"Mainstream media supports suburban morality!"

"I won't lie to you and say I don't have a classical name and a classical education. I know you take your names from flowers but you weren't born with them. Some of you probably were born with classical names…" Johnny began.

"Now, I'm a journalist. I'm bound by a code of conduct. I can't promise I can prove murder. I can't promise I won't prove your comrade was guilty. But I can say I believe that if you go on the record, then more of the truth will be known. That's all I can say I believe in. The truth for its own sake."

The flowerpunks went back to singing—their way of telling him to take a hike. He took the message and began to walk back to the student union. He wanted a cup of tea. He could drink it and think about how today was a failure.

The first floor of the student union contained a small cafe where an eighteen or nineteen-year-old student wearing a name tag that read: *Cleopatra* was working, despite the circumstances. Due to the faculty's sense of etiquette, she'd probably get paid.

Johnny ordered a small spiced tea and, as Cleopatra was about done making it, he was joined by a young woman in a white knee length dress. She was the very picture of suburban modesty. However, Johnny recognized her as one of the flowerpunks who'd rebuffed him earlier. Without the plastic yellow beret and blazer covered in dyed flowers, she could pass for a student. In fact, she probably was one.

"Orange juice with ginger and caffeine powder please." She ordered, and then turned her back to Cleopatra.

"Don't talk, just listen, you can quote me under the name Fern Cattail. The dead man was called Sunflower Jones. He was a little older than us and gay. When we were planning this march he confessed to me that Stross and he had been lovers. Stross told him he was simple neighborhood doctor, he didn't know Stross was even a genetics specialist until he accepted this job. Sunflower was heartbroken, but part of him couldn't believe it. He thought Stross was a cool person. Well, today he learned that love without peace is meaningless." She said it quickly and quietly.

"Just one question before you go, if I may. Sunflower's cane—I saw it, something like that costs a pretty penny, not something the average twenty-something could afford. Was it a gift from Professor Stross?"

"He said it was a gift from an old boyfriend, so it probably was. Wait a second do you mean..."

"If Stross gave him the cane, then Stross knew Sunflower

carried something he could claim was a weapon. If Sunflower had a weapon, Stross can plead self defense," Johnny replied. He tried to make it all sound like he was simply stating facts. He couldn't be seen as sympathetic to either Sunflower or Stross, but the old doctor really pissed him off.

Cleopatra returned with both of their drinks. Fern paid and said, "Keep the change." And Johnny was left to wonder what he should do next.

This changed things. If he managed to get some corroboration, this became a story of an ambitious doctor who was afraid of coming out of the closet. Not a big deal for a classicist, but to a macho man with watch connections it was social suicide.

Johnny quickly finished his spiced tea. He needed to be a little more proactive. The biology department was located in a large three and half story monstrosity at the edge of campus. The dean would likely still be in his office, as his honor would dictate, and Johnny was going to ambush him.

"Professor Ajax? My name is Johnny Orestes from *The Weekly Athenian*. I've uncovered some new information about the shooting that took place on campus earlier today and I was hoping to get a comment," Johnny called out knocking on the dean's door.

The elderly Professor Ajax opened the door just wide enough to peak out.

"If you know anything, go and tell the police. I'm quite busy," he huffed.

"I've learned that Stross and the dead man used to be lovers. Now, you hired Stross; did you know he was gay and had connections to the flowerpunk movement?"

"My dear boy, who isn't gay, bi or trans anymore? I told Stross to keep it in his pants and drop that young man 'Sundrop' or whatever his name was, along with his watch membership. But oh, no. No one listens to the old anymore. You can quote me on that!" Ajax showed surprising strength, like his namesake, and slammed the door.

The college's lawyers would probably claim that Ajax was old and under emotional duress or just deny that he'd admitted to knowing about the relationship. Johnny hadn't gotten it on tape and he regretted it.

Right now he had two options. He could go back to the student union and bang out a story on his phone about the right-wing professor who shot his ex-lover and the flowerpunks protesting his appointment, and hope he wasn't told it was "too sensational for a reputable news magazine" by his editor. Or he could turn his notes over to the state troopers and hope they were forwarded to a detective with the time to read them.

Or of course he could bluff like a basement gambler, which was in poor taste for a nice, classically educated, young man like himself.

Johnny found Stross sitting on a bench just outside the crime scene tape at the experimental garden. He was staring at the ground. *Guilt perhaps?* Johnny sat down next to him.

"Professor Stross, my name is Johnny Orestes from *The Weekly Athenian*. I don't want a quote from you, I just want you to listen. According to several sources, whose names I won't give up, I know that Sunflower Jones—the man you killed this afternoon—was your lover. I also know that the 'club' he supposedly came at you with was a gift from you to him, and more over I know that flowerpunks feel an almost religious connection to gardens even ones like this and he wouldn't have tarnished it with violence.

"It isn't hard to put together a likely story. You invited him here to talk, to tell him it was all a misunderstanding, and then when he was right in front of you—bang!—there goes any danger to your macho reputation. The thing is, all you had to do was embrace the classical lifestyle in your new profession and all this controversy would have blown over.

"Now I know a couple state police detectives through my work and I've already emailed them the bullet points of my story. Your best hope is to flee the jurisdiction." Johnny stood up and walked away feeling just safe enough to turn his back on Stross.

Johnny's story was watered down by the paper's lawyers to become a thought piece about whether or not stross believed Sunflower to be a neighborhood watchman, and whether or not he'd actually slept with a flowerpunk, allowing the reader to form their own opinion as to his innocence or guilt.

The bigger story that week was that Stross had resigned due to the controversy and announced he would go to the northern border to 'study in depth' cold climate pests. An easy place to flee—to the lawless Republic of Québec—if the need arose.

Originally hailing from mountainous Colorado CONNLYN SINCLAIR was raised by a sci-fi fangirl grandmother who let him read her collection of fantastical and mystery fiction as a teenager. These stories have since been much of the inspiration for his own work writing fantastic tales for both children and adults. He is currently studying to become a science teacher at KU. His soon to be released children's book is entitled, English & Scottish Fairy Tales of Francis James Child.

FROG JOY

PRE-RELEASE AVAILABLE NOW
HTTPS://ANAMCARA-PRESS.COM/

"Few brief, gem-like poetic meditations shine like Beth's. Part diary entry, part koan or prayer, these new poems sparkle with wit and wisdom. I treasure them. You will too."
—*Kevin Rabas, Past Poet Laureate of Kansas (2017-2019), Improvise*

Beth Gulley

Frog Joy is a collection of free verse and micro poems that point to the beauty in everyday moments. Beth Gulley is making her own world without a fence. Sometimes readers join her as she stains her fingers on low hanging mulberries. Other times the readers chase her along the trail and try to escape the rising flood waters. Underneath it all, a chorus of frog calls, like fingers running along the edge of a comb, echo in the damp night.

Subscribe to *The Write Bridge* Biannual Literary Journal

https://anamcara-press.com/
subscribe-to-the-journal/

Garden of Eden/Eatin':

Kevin Rabas

A Ten Minute Play

Characters:

Bertha: W, 72

Calvin: M, 21 (Bertha's grandson)

Time and place:

1995. A bare stage with semblances of a diner.

Props:

Chairs and blocks.

Synopsis:

In this light drama, a young man goes to visit his grandmother in the small town of Lucas, Kansas, home of sculptor S.P. Dinsmoor's Garden of Eden. The young man comes hoping to take a picture of the sculpture garden and reconnect with his grandmother and his family history. The grandmother tells him a secret about Dinsmoor and his garden, and sends him, somewhat changed, home.

BERTHA

I'm not goin'.

CALVIN

I'd like you to come with me. You know the place so well. Show me around.

BERTHA

I don't like that place. (beat) Is that what brought you all up this way, hon—you wanna tour of old Dinsmoore's sculpture garden? You didn't come to see your ole Grandma?

CALVIN

Oh, I always love seeing you, Grandma Bert. But I'm also on assignment. I've come to take photos of the Garden of Eden. For school. For photography class at college. I remember the sculptures being so beautiful at sunset.

BERTHA

And strange.

CALVIN

And I thought it'd be nice to see you, too, Grandma Bert.

BERTHA

But what is it, four hours—on a weeknight? Don't you have school? Big city school?

CALVIN

Oh, it's college, Grandma. I never get much sleep. Some of the kids don't believe this place exists. They may never know how strange—and wonderful—it is. So, I thought I'd show them, take some pictures, bring it back on film. Please go with me to see it this evening?

BERTHA

I don't like that place.

CALVIN

But it's the Garden of Eden. Haven't folks been coming to Lucas for decades to see it, isn't it what the town's known for?

BERTHA

That and gossip. And this K-18 Café. Dunderheads decided to rename it.

 (together) CALVIN & BERTHA

Garden of Eatin'.

CALVIN

(joking) Good eatin' at the Garden of Eatin'. Lucas, Kansas, USA.

BERTHA

Where's your grammar, son? Aren't you supposed to be an English major at that big city, Kansas City college?

CALVIN

It's ok to be colloquial. It's ok to talk like normal folks.

BERTHA

That ain't bad. That ain't half bad. Respect your roots. But don't let me catch you wearin' your pants backwards or wearin' your pants down at your knees. I ain't used to seein' young men's underthings. Those times are passed. My boys is grown. You listen to rap, all that?

CALVIN

Not much. I like jazz.

BERTHA

Kan-sas Ciiiity. Ain't it just all up to date in that there Kansas City?

CALVIN

Somewhat. Most of it.

BERTHA

You too big for here? Too big for sittin' with your grandma at the K-18 Café?

CALVIN

Not at all. Wanted to see the place. See you. See the beauty of the place.

BERTHA

And the darkness. The strange?

CALVIN

Come with me, will ya? I'd like to see Eden again?

BERTHA

You can go without me. I've seen it. You know, I live here. See it everyday as I cross to the grocery. Never go in.

CALVIN

Why not?

BERTHA

I have my reasons.

CALVIN

Tell me about them.

BERTHA

Oh, nothing much. I knew him.

CALVIN

Dinsmoor?

BERTHA

Yes. He wasn't always an artist, you know? He was a man in our town. Strange man. Peculiar man. What we'd call an odd duck.

CALVIN

How?

BERTHA

He was a short fellow. Little Tom Thumb. Maybe 5'2". He rode around on a white horse brought from back east in a white suit.

CALVIN

Like Colonel Sanders?

BERTHA

That's it. Like that city Southern chicken guy. Nobody liked him much 'til he started building. Then they all came. He had electric lights, you know? Had a generator. Here we were with our oil lamps at night, and he has the place lit up like a Christmas tree.

CALVIN

It must have been something.

BERTHA

Damn trains started stoppin' here. Everybody getting' off at our stop—to see the lights, see the sculptors, and that crazy ole hoot preachin' about his God, about Adam and Eve, Cain and Abel. Cain there with his potato hoe, slappin' Abel up side the head, knockin' him dead. Ole Dinsmoor must've liked that story.

CALVIN

How'd you know him?

BERTHA

Everybody knew him. Crazy ole coot. I fed his animals.

CALVIN

Animals?

BERTHA.

He kept badgers. Turkeys. Even an eagle. He used them animals as models. For his art.

CALVIN

Sculpted them?

BERTHA

Yep. Sculpted them. Put a turkey up there with an 'merican flag. Said that was the better bird. Big wing blew 'em down, bird and concrete flag. He just kept puttin' them up there again, against the wind.

CALVIN

What'd it look like at first?

BERTHA

Wasn't much. Just that log cabin made out of concrete logs. Later, he started puttin' up them poles, most of them 40 foot. Then he hoisted up the sculptures. And he weren't trained. Everything was just from him. And he weren't young.

CALVIN

How old was he?

BERTHA

Sixty-four I think, when he started. Him and a colored fellow. Just the two them. In a few years, it was all mostly up, them sculptures, them creepy sculptures, and Adam in his loin cloth. He didn't start like that. Town made him put that on. At first, you could see everything, their privates. Not in this town.

CALVIN

It seems like it's loosing steam, like rain's taking the statues.

BERTHA

Sure is. He used a special mixture. Native limestone in it. No one knows the mixture. No one knows the mortar. So, the arms are falling off of Cain. Eve's breasts are crumbling. The snake's fallin' clean apart.

CALVIN

Come with me.

BERTHA

No, sonny. No can do. I've been there before. Been there, seen it.

CALVIN

But you know it better than almost everyone else. You could help me see it with new eyes.

BERTHA

Sure. Better than most. But I have my reasons.

CALVIN

Tell me why.

BERTHA

Like I said, as a girl I knew him. Fed his animals. Sundays, before church, I'd bring his badgers a handful of gingersnaps. He's there, you know. Dinsmoor's still there. You can see him.

CALVIN

You mean, like Lenin, behind glass? In the ziggurat?

BERTHA

Yes. And that's the reason I'm not going in. I remember him. I don't want to see him like that.

CALVIN

I'm sorry. That must be hard.

BERTHA

We went once. When I was an older girl. We went to see him. A man handed me a flashlight, and we walked into the dark, and there he was, behind glass. His face was like a glove. There'd been a crack in the glass, and he was losing to it. Damn face turnin' to dust right in front of us. But he was the same. Kinda small, but handsome for a man. And I can remember him talkin' through that tube, sermonizin' to anyone who'd listen, speakin' from behind his sculptures. I liked him, and now he's gone.

CALVIN

Gone.

BERTHA

But his damn body's still here with us. Maybe hasn't even passed on. Won't go away. No, sonny, I ain't comin' with ya. I'll stay here. Eat some flapjacks with ya, but I ain't goin' in. Ain't goin' too near that place. I know it's in our town, but it ain't our whole town. It ain't us. It's just him. It's just Dinsmoor sleeping, sleepin' the long sleep of death. And I want no part of it. Don't want no reminder of where we're all goin', and how he's just lyin' flat there, rottin' away.

CALVIN

I'm sorry. I should have—

BERTHA

No, it's ok, sonny. You couldn't've known. To the town, you're just another tourist lookin' to get a glimpse of Eden how Dinsmoor saw it. You'll come and go, but Eden stays. As my pappy used to say, "You know where I live, just a few steps from Eden. Up the way's Paradise, and you go down about a mile, and you end up in Hell Crick." Damn strange way of namin' things, round here. Sounds like we all walked right out of the Good Book, doesn't it?

CALVIN

Sure does.

BERTHA

But we didn't. We're just as forward and backward as anyone else, out here, in the center, where there's wheat all around.

CALVIN

Come with me. Once.

BERTHA

Forget it, kid. Forget all about it. Take your pictures and go home. I'll send you your letters at Christmas and for your birthday. It's ok. We love you. Don't worry about us out here in Eden. Go on home.

BLACKOUT

KEVIN RABAS, http://kevinrabas.com/ Past Poet Laureate of Kansas (2017-2019) Kevin Rabas teaches at Emporia State University, where he leads the poetry and playwriting tracks in the Department of English, Modern Languages, and Journalism. He is a seventh generation Kansan. He has fourteen books, including Lisa's Flying Electric Piano, a Kansas Notable Book and Nelson Poetry Book Award winner. He is the recipient of the Emporia State President's and Liberal Arts & Sciences Awards for Research and Creativity, and he is the winner of the Langston Hughes Award for Poetry.

Glendyn Buckley, Author, and Barbara Waterman-Peters, Author, Illustrator

BARBARA WATERMAN PETERS

Interview With An Artist

BARBARA WATERMAN PETERS
ARTIST, ILLUSTRATER, AUTHOR

— BY MICKI CARROLL

MC: Of all the vehicles available for expression, why did you choose the media you use?

BW-P: I utilize many different media, but oils and watercolors most often. I find them to be more responsive to my aesthetic.

MC: How many paintings have you created? Which is your favorite?

BW-P: I have created thousands of works. Although I have no favorite, there are a few which I consider to be "signature" pieces.

MC: Can you tell about an early experience where you learned that art had power?

BW-P: In the early 1990s I was working on the beginning of my women series (MWS). The figures were surrealistic as I was exploring relationships between and among women in families. I was invited to show them in another city. During the exhibition someone demanded fruitlessly they be removed as they were "satanic." That same experience happened again elsewhere, and that time I had to take down the show.

MC: What are some words you despise that have been used to describe your artwork by others?

BW-P: Of all your questions, this is the one I have found most difficult to answer. My surrealist works reminded one viewer of "Halloween." "So, what" was directed at one of my paintings by an art professor. A couple of art critics in Kansas City said some things that stung. However, both had found the work at least worthy of writing about, and one had reproduced one of my paintings in full color above the fold on page one of the ARTS section in the Kansas City Star to demonstrate why she hated it! I, of course, was thrilled.

MC: Is there anything special about your art studio or space or process that you think helps you?

BW-P: I have two studios. One is in my home and takes up half of our lower level. (My husband has a studio in the other half.) I do watercolors, drawings, and other works here. My second studio is in the North Topeka Arts & Entertainment District (NOTO). There I concentrate on my oil painting. I find that having these dedicated spaces helps me focus.

MC: What would you say is the most difficult part of creating art?

BW-P: Of course, the technical aspects present endless challenges, but the most difficult is prioritizing my art over daily concerns. My studio away from home helps with that.

MC: What do you enjoy most about creating art?

BW-P: I can act upon my ideas, bring them to a tangible form, and share my concepts with others. But more than that is the actual experience of drawing lines, brushing colors, and seeing the magic happen. I never tire of that.

MC: What is something surprising you learned about yourself through creating art?

BW-P: That I can rise to the occasion and stretch my aesthetic muscles. In short, finding myself more capable than I realized.

MC: Do you hide any secrets in your artwork that only a few people will find?

BW-P: Oh yes, particularly in my political works. But I include subtle nuances and references in other series, too.

MC: What does success look like to you?

BW-P: Shows and sales rank highly but having my viewers "get" my work and want to discuss it, write about it, or pair it with their own creative endeavors is marvelous.

MC: Do you view art creation as a kind of spiritual practice?

BW-P: By any measurement the Arts are spiritual experiences both for the creator and the audience. But to your question: the act of creating allows a portal into another realm, another dimension which is often called "the zone." There is no time, no pain, no awareness of the physical world. What is there is the freedom to explore all sorts of possibilities and even some impossibilities.

MC: Who are some of your favorite artists?

BW-P: I admire the works of many artists both living and dead. Some, like Caravaggio, have deeply influenced my painting. A favorite contemporary painter is Andrea Kowch.

MC: Who or what turned you on to painting?

BW-P: A family member gave me an oil painting set when I was twelve. I was hooked.

MC: Are you originally from Kansas?

BW-P: Yes. I was born in Topeka. I have, however, lived in New Jersey, New York, New Mexico, and Texas.

MC: Do you feel compelled to create? Why? How?

BW-P: Sometimes the urge to draw, paint, or write is as strong as the need to eat. New ideas are hard taskmasters, but so are half-finished works which continue to demand attention. Ironically, I forget to eat when the Muse is cracking her whip!

MC: How many hours a day/week do you "do art"?

BW-P: It varies, but if I can spend one or two hours of writing in the morning and four or five productive hours painting during the afternoon, I am pleased.

MC: If you didn't do art, what would you do?

BW-P: Years ago, I worked in banking which I enjoyed.

MC: Do you try to be more original or more traditional as an artist?

BW-P: This is an interesting question and one that would take an essay to answer, but perhaps I can simplify by saying I utilize traditional media to express my original concepts.

MC: Do you want each piece to stand on its own, or are you trying to build a body of work with connections between each creation?

BW-P: I like to work in series, enabling me to explore variations and fresh challenges within the parameters. Sometimes a series might occupy me for ten to more than twenty years. My Map Series and My Women Series are examples. Other works could be grouped in categories rather than series, such as my landscapes, florals, and portraits. I do occasionally create a "one-off" for a commission or just for fun. As an interesting aside, a piece from my Fantastic Pond Series launched my career as a children's book illustrator!

MC: If you could talk to your younger artist self, what advice would you give?

BW-P: The best advice I would give myself would be to focus more on specific goals right after getting my undergraduate degree. While continuing to paint and show my work, I did not really find my path for about five years!

MC: How did your first art show change your process of creating?

BW-P: My first important solo exhibit was in 1981, but by then my work had already been in galleries and national juried shows for a couple of years. All of this was validation and incentive to work even harder.

MC: Do you have relationships with other artists? How do you support each other?

BW-P: My husband, Larry Peters, is an artist. He works in ceramics, sculpture, and collage. My daughter is a fine art photographer. I own STUDIO 831 in NOTO and rent studio space to other artists. I was a founding member of The Collective, an artists' co-op, and a charter member of Circle of 7. I enjoy friendships and networking with artists across Kansas and beyond. I consider myself an Arts advocate as well.

MC: How do you balance your time creating art with your time promoting your art?

BW-P: This is an ongoing challenge! Generally, as I stated

earlier, early morning is reading poetry and writing; late morning, emails, and business matters; afternoon studio work. However, this ideal set-up does not always work, so a certain amount of flexibility is required. Facebook is great for self-promotion, but so is being open to other opportunities such as community involvement in the Arts. Marketing is more than purchasing advertising space although that is a good one!

MC: Do you finish everything you create? What happens to old starts?

BW-P: I tend to finish what I start. That being said, I have unframed canvases, flat files full of unmatted works on paper, and notebooks with never-to-be published writing. Usually, these are second string pieces which don't merit the cost of framing, matting, or submission. Or there are simply too many of them such as figure studies and preparatory sketches. One exception is my unsuccessful watercolors. Because they are done on expensive paper and have areas of beautiful color, I tear them up and my husband and I use them in other works.

MC: Do you have any recommendations for young or aspiring artists?

BW-P: My very long career has taught me many things, but these stand out: hard work, constant study and research, self-discipline, attention to detail, respect for your own work, craftsmanship, respect for the work of others, being open to opportunities, and networking. There are NO shortcuts.

Barbara Waterman-Peters, (BFA, Washburn University, MFA, Kansas State University, Honorary Doctor of Fine Arts, Washburn University) has works in museum and corporate collections, and shows in several galleries. She has shown regionally, nationally, and internationally in more than 350 solo, invitational and juried exhibitions. Her artwork has been included in *Kansas Speaks Out, Writing from the Center, The Write Bridge, Inscape,* and *Flint Hills Review* as well as on the covers of numerous books.

She owns Pen & Brush Press along with Glendyn Buckley. Together they have created and published three children's books and are working on a fourth.

Her writing has been published in *105 Meadowlark Reader, The Writer's Place Yearbook, Kansas Speaks Out, Kansas Reflector, The Write Bridge,* and All Over the Map, an Anthology among others. She writes about art and artists for *Topeka Magazine.*

Bookstores Carrying
The Write Bridge Journal

Ad Astra Books & Coffee House, 135 N Santa Fe Ave, Salina KS 67501; 785-833-2235

Barney Loves Books, 22 S Main Street, Woodstown, New Jersey; 856-624-4723

Crow & Co. Books, 2 S Main St., Hutchinson KS 67501; 620-500-5200

Flint Hills Books, 130 W. Main · Council Grove, Kansas 66846; 620-767-5054

Monarch Books & Gifts, 7713 W. 151st Street, Overland Park, KS; 913-766-8646

Prosperos Books & Media, 1800 W 39th St,Kansas City, MO 64111; (816) 531-9673

The Raven Bookstore, 809 Massachusetts St, Lawrence, KS 66044; 785-749-3300

Rivendell Bookstore, 212 N Broadway St, Abilene, KS 67410; 785-571-5001

Roundtable bookstore, 826 N Kansas Ave, Topeka, KS 66608; 785-329-5366

Twice Told Tales, 104 S Main St, McPherson KS 67460; 620-718-5023

Watermark Books & Café, 4701 E Douglas, Wichita, KS 67218; 316-682-1181. www.watermarkbooks.com

Ask your local bookstore to carry **The Write Bridge** Journal!

Resources for
Writers

ARTISTS & ILLUSTRATORS

Bobbie Powell, bobbielynpowell@gmail.com, https://www.facebook.com/php?id=10064184227637

Cathy Martin, McLouth, Kansas, cymn4art@gmail.com

Amanda McCollum, Overland Park, Kansas.

Diana Dunkley, Studio 3D, 1019 Delaware St., Lawrence, Kansas USA 66044, ddunkleyat3d@earthlink.net

PRINTERS

KC Book Manufacturing Co. 110 W 12th Ave, Kansas City, MO 64116; (816) 842-9770

Bookmobile, 210 Edge Place, Minneapolis, MN 55418,

Gasch Printing, 1780 Crossroads Dr, Odenton, MD 21113

Oklahoma Bindery, Inc., 2832 W. Lindley, Oklahoma City, OK 73107

Mennonite Press, Inc., 532 N. Oliver Road, Newton, KS 67114, BetterSelf-Publishing.com 800-536-4686

Thanks To Our Sponsors:

Thaddeus Dugan

Amber Fraley

George Gurley

Dennis Hargis

Duane L. Herrmann

Debra Irsik

Jewelry By Julie

Kathleen Kaska

Bruce Rolfe

Barbara Waterman Peters

Subscribe to *The Write Bridge* Biannual Literary Journal

https://anamcara-press.com/
subscribe-to-the-journal/

The Write Bridge journal has showcased over 140 writers on a variety of topics since 2021. Issue #6, *Solitude & Solidarity*, is available in both print *and* online at: https://anamcara-press.com/the-write-bridge-zine/

The Write Bridge online Zine is complementary. Please enjoy the 60 + page limited – but full-color – online Zine and share with your friends!

The Write Bridge unabridged print journal is an approximately 200 page paperback with all of your favorite, and soon to be favorite authors and artists from across the Heartland and beyond.

We are partnering with independent bookstores, libraries, and specialty shops to spread *The Write Bridge* far and wide! We hope you'll help us in our effort to broadcast this seed.

How can you help? Read and subscribe! Also…

- Ask your local library to subscribe.
- Share *The Write Bridge* with your friends and on social media
- Submit to our next issue of *The Write Bridge*
- Advertise in the next issue
- Contact your favorite author in the journal and tell them what you liked about their writing.

Submit your writing to the write bridge print and online journal:

SUMMER 2024 TOPIC: GRIEF and COMFORT
DEADLINE: MAY 31, 2024